Carol Yeh-Yun Lin · Leif Edvinsson
Jeffrey Chen · Tord Beding

National Intellectual Capital and the Financial Crisis in Indonesia, Malaysia, The Philippines, and Thailand

Springer

Carol Yeh-Yun Lin
Department of Business Administration
National Chengchi University
Taipei
Taiwan

Leif Edvinsson
Universal Networking Intellectual Capital
Norrtälje
Sweden

Jeffrey Chen
Accenture
Chicago, IL
USA

Tord Beding
TC-Growth AB
Karlstad
Sweden

ISSN 2191-5504 ISSN 2191-5512 (electronic)
ISBN 978-1-4614-7942-0 ISBN 978-1-4614-7943-7 (eBook)
DOI 10.1007/978-1-4614-7943-7
Springer New York Heidelberg Dordrecht London

Library of Congress Control Number: 2013940091

Printed on acid-free paper

Springer is part of Springer Science+Business Media (www.springer.com)

Foreword I

The economic crisis is a consequence of many parallel factors which are all related to globalization and digitalization. My main concern, assessing this in more detail from the European perspective, is that revolutionary global forces have not been taken early nor seriously enough by most national and regional decision makers. The Heads of European States and Governments have once again recalled the importance of fiscal consolidation, structural reform, and targeted investment to put Europe back on the path of smart, sustainable, and inclusive growth. The main question is how capable and ready are the national governments to tackling the complex and manifold issues of crises and to renewing even radically many of our public and private structures and processes.

The first basic requirement is that all the European Union Member States remain fully committed to taking the actions required at the national level to achieve the objectives of the Europe 2020 Strategy. The second basic requirement is that the national and regional governments, as well as people, are ready for radical changes. This booklet, and the other 11 booklets by the experienced authors, focus on National intellectual capital (NIC) and give necessary insights and facts for us the readers and especially for our in-depth systemic thinking of the interrelationships of NIC and economic recovery.

How should the national and regional decision makers tackle the existing knowledge of intangible capital? The focus needs to be more on the bottom-up approach stressing the developments on local and regional levels. I highlight our recent statements by the EU Committee of the Regions. The key priorities are to get more innovations out of research and to encourage mindset change towards open innovation.

Political decision makers are finally aware that the traditional indicators created for and used in industrial production cannot be applied to a knowledge intensive, turbulent, and innovativeness-based global enterprise environment. Indicators that perceive the intangible dimensions of competitiveness—knowledge capital, innovation knowledge, and anticipation of the future—have been developed around the world, but their use has not yet become established in practice. This booklet accelerates the development and the use of these indicators.

This helps the local and regional, as well as central, governments in taking brave leaps forward on a practical level—giving greater ownership and involving all the stakeholders. This means the need of actions towards increasing the structural and relational capital of regions, both internally in communities of practice and in collaboration with others.

The new generation innovation activities are socially motivated, open, and collectively participated, complex and global by nature. The regions need to move towards open innovation, within a human-centered vision of partnerships between public and private sector actors, with universities playing a crucial role.

Regions should be encouraged to develop regional innovation platforms, which act as demand-based service centres and promote the use of international knowledge to implement the Europe 2020 Strategy, smart specialization, and European partnerships according to the interests and needs of regions. For this to happen, we need to apply the new dynamic understanding of regional innovation ecosystems, in which companies, cities, and universities, as well as other public and private sector actors (the "Triple Helix") learn to work together in new and creative ways to fully harness their innovative potential.

New innovative practices do not come about by themselves. One major potential is the use of public procurement. The renewing of the European wide rules must increase the strategic agility and activities of municipalities and other public operators as creators of new solutions. Especially, the execution of pre-commercial procurement should be reinforced even more in combination with open innovation to speed-up the green knowledge society development, i.e., for common re-usable solutions in creating the infrastructures and services modern real-world innovation ecosystems are built upon. Conditions must be created that also allow for extensive development projects which address complex societal challenges and which take the form of risk-taking consortia.

One of our working instruments within the Committee of the Regions is the Europe 2020 Monitoring Platform, which broadly reviews and reflects the opinions and decisions on regional level all around Europe. It gives a flavor of cultural and other socio economic differences inside the EU. This brings an important perspective to the intellectual capital, namely the values and attitudes needed for citizens supporting policymakers on appropriate long-term investments and policies.

Emphasizing the importance of these issues, decision makers in all countries and regions worldwide need a deep and broad understanding of the critical success factors affecting the NIC. With all the facts and frames for thinking, this booklet gives a valuable insight in today's challenges.

Markku Markkula
Advisor to the Aalto University Presidents
Member of the EU Committee of the Regions
Former Member of the Parliament of Finland

Foreword II

Financial crisis—words very much heard today. What is all this about, actually, and how to get a grip on what we experience today? The booklet gives an important insight on the factors affecting competitiveness and productivity in modern knowledge society. We need to see behind the obvious, and we need to have increasingly "qualified guesses" as the character of the society and industry has fundamentally changed.

What is very important to notice is the shift towards intangible value creation beyond the deterministic phenomena we saw very clearly in the industrial era. Cost drivers were the important ones throughout the industry. Mass production, bigger is better; very traditional productivity factors, was the mantra.

However, the production picture is changing. Increasingly, value is created by the intangibles, often services related to the tangible components, and even totally in immaterial value creation, where perceptions and expectations determine the market value of the "extended product". We also see rapid change in organizational forms, We see new type of entrepreneurship growing besides the traditional industry clusters, we see smart specialization of regions and countries.

This means also that there will be clearly different and complementary roles of the actors in innovation and value creation ecosystems. Large companies, small ones and even microenterprises together with the public sector are traditionally seen as the active partners in such innovation environments. The real issue in the dynamic markets is however that the end users are increasingly to be taken on board as *active subjects* for innovation, and not merely treated as objects, customers. Markets need to be shaped and created in much more dynamic way than ever before. Open innovation beyond cross-licensing includes the societal capital as an important intangible engine for productivity growth. Innovation happens only when the offering is meeting the demand. Otherwise, we can only speak about inventions or ideas…

We need to have a close look at the intellectual capital and the different factors within it when we design our policy approaches. Short-term investments in process capital (infrastructures) and market capital seem to be very important for the manufacturing base as such, but at the same time measures for longer term intellectual capital development and efficiency need to be taken.

Increasingly important is the *structure* and the open *processes* related to intangible capital and knowledge pools. For sustainable long-term development both the *human capital and renewal capital are crucial*, as they are directly related to the innovation capability of the region. The correlation between these factors and the GDP growth is undisputable. In knowledge intense industries talent is attracting talent, and the connectivity which modern ICT provides makes this talent pool fluid across disciplines, organizations, and geographical settings. It is imperative to modernize the innovation systems enabling the full dynamics needed for success in knowledge intense industries, beyond the traditional boundaries.

Measuring performance of innovation systems becomes increasingly complex due to the mash-up of different disciplines, having new types of actors, and interactions between them. Hence, the importance of analysis of the various components of the national intellectual capital (NIC) (and equally on national innovation capability) as done in this booklet cannot be underestimated when making qualified guesses for operational choices to create functioning innovation ecosystems. The only predictable in true innovation is the unpredictability and the surprises. The role of the public sector is to drive strategy and measures enabling the unpredictable, and to catalyze a fluid, seamless, and frictionless innovation system to grow, with strong interplay with the surrounding society.

We need to have courage to experiment, to prototype in real-world settings, to have all stakeholders involved to find and remove the friction points of innovation and to achieve sustainable innovation ecosystems for knowledge intensive products and services.

I wish you interesting reading with this mind opening report.

Bror Salmelin
Advisor, Innovation Systems
European Commission
DG CONNECT

Foreword III

The 2008 global financial crisis hit the whole world with unprecedented speed, causing widespread financial panic. Consumer confidence dropped to the lowest level since the Great Depression. Taiwan, with an export-dependent economy, was seriously impacted by the crisis and the unemployment rate hiked while household consumption levels dropped. At the onset of the financial crisis, Prof. Lin was the Dean of Student Affairs here at National Chengchi University in Taipei, Taiwan. She was the dean in charge of financial aid and student loans and thus saw firsthand the direct impact the financial crisis had upon our students. The crisis was so devastating that Prof. Lin, along with the university, was compelled to launch several new initiatives to raise money, and help students weather the difficult times.

I am very glad that she took this painful experience to heart and set herself upon the task of investigating the impact of the crisis; trying to look into the causes and consequences for policy implications, not only for Taiwan but for an array of 48 countries. In particular, she approaches the crisis from the perspective of "national intellectual capital (NIC)" which is very important in today's knowledge-driven economy.

Taiwan is an example of a knowledge economy and has enjoyed the fame of being referred to as a "high-tech island." Without an abundance of natural resources, Taiwan's hardworking and highly educated population is the single most precious resource that the island has. Acknowledging the value of such human resources and intellectual capital, we established the Taiwan Intellectual Capital Research Center (TICRC) under my leadership in 2003. Ever since then, Taiwan's government has continuously funded the university to conduct relevant research projects aimed at enhancing the intellectual capital of Taiwan. Having been thus endowed with the responsibility of nourishing future leaders in the public and private sectors, we have focused on building up our strength in innovation, entrepreneurship, and technology management-related research and education.

To enhance intellectual capital research, we recently formed a joint team of professors for a 4-year project in order to leverage their respective research capabilities. Through this project we hope to provide policy suggestions for the government by exploring the creativity, innovation, and intellectual capital at national, regional, city, and county levels. The goal is to come up with an intangible assets (IA) agenda for Taiwan's future sustainability. Professor Lin is an integral member in this research team.

Following her 2011 book *National Intellectual Capital: A Comparison of 40 Countries*, this booklet series is Prof. Lin's second attempt at presenting her research, conducted under the sponsorship of TICRC, to international readers. As the Founding Director of TICRC and her President, I am honored to give a brief introduction of the value of this booklet series.

In comparison to her 2011 book, this series increased the number of countries studied to 48, and particularly focuses on the impact of intellectual capital on the 2008 global financial crisis. Rarely has an economic issue been systematically studied from the view point of IA, particularly at such a large scale of 48 countries. The research results show without a doubt that NIC is indeed an important economic development enhancer. In particular, the fact that countries with higher national intellectual capital experienced faster recoveries from the 2008 financial crisis provides a strong message for the policymakers.

In addition to providing insights to national policy, the booklet also summarizes the background of each country before the crisis, the key events during the crisis, economic development afterwards, and future prospects and challenges. Each volume affords readers a holistic picture of what happened in each country in an efficient manner. The linkage between NIC and this financial crisis also provides a different perspective of the crisis.

We are happy that Prof. Lin continues to share her valuable research results with international readers. I sincerely hope that her insights can garner more attention concerning the benefits of developing NIC for the well-being of every nation.

Se-Hwa Wu
Professor, Graduate Institute of Technology
and Innovation Management
President, National Chengchi University
Taipei, Taiwan

Preface I

There are "mounting risks of a breakup of the Euro zone." Such comments are frequent today on how the European leaders are handling the escalating crisis and its potential impact on non-European countries. But few leaders, reporters, or researchers are actually addressing the situation of national intellectual capital (NIC) and its signals. In addition to the financial crisis, is there an emerging NIC crisis as well? Why is it emerging? How should policymakers think about NIC? In what way does it need specific attention? When will the outcome and impact of taken NIC policy steps be realized?

In the midst of the European crisis, there are national interventions to address the issues mentioned above. In leading economical nations the investments going into intangibles now exceeds tangibles, and is positively correlated to income per capita. However, these still do not show up clearly in national mapping as well as policy making insights. Therefore, the New Club of Paris is focusing the knowledge agenda setting for countries on Societal Innovation (see www.new-club of-paris.org).

Chairman Ben Bernanke of the U.S. Federal Reserve was addressing some of these same aspects in a key note speech in May 2011 hosted by Georgetown University: http://www.icapitaladvisors.com/2011/05/31/bernanke-on-intangible-capital/. OECD and the World Bank are developing NIC statistics, often based on the model from Corrado-Hultén. Japan has been developing both NIC and Intangible Assets (IA) at METI for some time now. Their research on IC/IA has resulted in a National IA Week with various key stakeholders, such as government agencies, universities, stock exchange, and enterprises. Japan is so far the only country in the world to hold such activities, and they have been doing so for the last 8 years. Australia, Singapore, South Korea, and China are currently undertaking various NIC initiatives. Other countries are also becoming more and more aware of NIC, with policy rhetoric centered on innovation, education, R&D, and trade. Despite this, the map for a more justified NIC navigation has been missing.

This booklet highlights NIC development for a number of countries, based on 48 different indicators, aggregated into four major NIC components of human capital, market capital, process capital, and renewal capital. The model here is a refined and verified statistical model in comparison to the Corrado-Hultén model. We call it the L–E–S model after the contributors Lin–Edvinsson–Stahle. Based on a deeper understanding and the timeline pattern it sets forth, this model will add to a better NIC navigation, not to mention knowledge agenda setting for countries.

Upon looking at a global cluster NIC map, it is evident that the top leading countries seem to be small countries, especially Singapore, the Nordic countries, Hong Kong, and Taiwan. For the U.S., Finland, and Sweden around 50 % or more of its economical growth is related to NIC aspects. Sweden, Finland, Switzerland, the U.S., Israel, and Denmark are strongly influenced in its GDP growth by focusing on Renewal Capital.

It might be that we will see a clearer map of the NIC ecosystem and drivers for wealth emerge in the extension of this ongoing unique research of NIC. This booklet will present a NIC map for various clusters of countries. It can be used for bench marking as well as bench learning for policy prototyping. The starting point is awareness and thinking of NIC, and its drivers for economic results. Based on this more refined navigation, NIC metrics can be presented.

Deeper understanding will emerge from this research, such as the scaling up of limited skilled human capital in one nation by using the globalized broadband technologies for migration and flow of knowledge (such as tele-medicine or mobile banking in Africa). This is also referred to as the IC multiplier. It might also be the way the old British Commonwealth was constructed, but without the IC taxonomy. In modern taxonomy it might be the shaping of NIC alliances for the migration and flow of IC between nations?

Another understanding that might emerge for policy making is the issue of employment versus unemployment. The critical understanding will be deployment of IC drivers. This will require another networked workforce of value networkers on a global scale, such as volunteering software and apps developers. However such volunteers do not show up in traditional statistics, for the mapping on behalf of policymakers.

On another level there might be a clear gap analyses between nations to support the vision process of a nation. On a deeper level it is also a leadership responsibility to address the gap of NIC positions versus potential positions. Such a gap is in fact a liability to the citizens, to be addressed in due time.

This will take us to the need for the continuous renewal of social systems. The so called Arab Spring is explained by some as resulting from three drivers: lack of renewal of social systems, Internet, and soccer as cross class interaction space. The lack of social renewal and innovation is most likely critical early warning signals. For Greece, we can see such a tipping point occurred back in 1999.

On a global scale we might see that the concern for the Euro zone crisis should and can be explained by a deeper and supplementary understanding of NIC, in addition to financial capital. So we need to refine our NIC understanding, NIC mapping, NIC metrics, and NIC organizational constructs into societal innovation for the benefit of wealth creation of subsequent generations.

Leif Edvinsson
The World's First Professor of Intellectual Capital
Chairman and Co-founder of New Club of Paris

Preface II

Our first book *National Intellectual Capital: A Comparison of 40 Countries* was published in early 2011, at a time when the 2008 global financial crisis had been declared over yet the European region was still plagued with sovereign debt problems. Before we finalized the book, we were able to retrieve some of our raw data concerning the troubled countries, such as Greece, Iceland, Ireland, Portugal, and Spain. The results of our analysis based on data spanning 1995–2008 revealed some early warning signs of the financial turmoil in those countries. In my preface of that book, I mentioned the warning signs might reveal only the tip of an iceberg. At that time, my co-author, Prof. Edvinsson and I decided to do a follow-up study to trace the development of National Intellectual Capital (NIC) in as many countries as possible, particularly through the lens of the 2008 global financial crisis. This 12 booklet series is the result of that determination.

The 2008 global financial crisis came with unexpected speed and had such a wide-spread effect that surprised many countries far from the epicenter of the initial U.S. sub-prime financial problem, geographically and financially. According to reports, no country was immune from the impact of this financial crisis. Such development clearly signifies how closely connected the world has become and the importance of having a global interdependent view. By reporting what happened during 2005–2010 in 48 major countries throughout the world, this booklet series serves the purpose of uncovering national problems before the crisis, government coping strategies, stimulus plans, potential prospects and challenges of each individual country, and the interdependence between countries. The 6 years of data allow us to compare NIC and economic development crossing before, during, and after the financial crisis. They are handy booklets for readers to have a quick yet overall view of countries of personal interest. The list of 48 countries in 11 clusters is provided in the appendix of each booklet.

Searching for financial crisis-related literature for 48 countries is itself a very daunting task, not to mention summarizing and analyzing it. For financial crisis related literature, we mainly relied on the reports and statistics of certain world organizations, including OECD, World Bank, United Nations, International Monetary Fund (IMF), European Commission Office, the US Congressional Research Service, the U.S. Central Intelligence Agency, and International Labor

Office (ILO). Some reliable research centers, such as the National Bureau of Economic Research in the U.S., World Economic Forum, the Heritage Foundation in the U.S., and government websites from each country were also our sources of information. Due to the requirement of more update and comprehensive information, we were not able to use as much academic literature as we would have liked, because it generally covers a very specific topic with time lag and with research methods not easily comprehended by the general public. Therefore, we had to resort to some online news reports for more current information.

In the middle of 2012, the lasting financial troubles caused the European economy to tilt back into a recession, which also slowed down economic growth across the globe. However almost 4 years have passed since the outbreak of the global financial crisis in late 2008; it is about time to reflect on what happened and the impact of the financial crisis. By comparing so many countries, we came to a preliminary conclusion that countries with faster recovery from the financial crisis have higher NIC than those with slower recovery. In other words, countries that rebounded fast from the crisis generally have solid NIC fundamentals, including human capital, market capital, process capital, and renewal capital. We also found that the higher the NIC, the higher the GDP per capital (ppp). This booklet series provides a different perspective to look beyond the traditional economic indicators for national development.

In an era when IA have become a key competitive advantage, investing in NIC development is investing in future national development and well-being

Enjoy!

Carol Yeh-Yun Lin
Professor, Department of Business Adminstration
National Chengchi University, Taiwan
Taiwan Intellectual Capital Research Center (TICRC)

Executive Summary

Establishing a regional supporting system is an effective way to combat financial crisis.

How can national intellectual capital (NIC) be supportive as a policy guideline for national well-being? A key factor in the financial crisis was the conventional financial system failed to detect potential risks due to non-transparent information disclosure. Our earlier NIC research has revealed certain warning signs of impending financial crisis for Greece, Iceland, and Ireland. Such findings indicate that NIC, albeit intangible, can provide valuable insights into future risk control and strategy formulation. This booklet looks into the connections between the 2008 global financial crisis and NIC development. It briefly reports the main causes of why these four countries were dragged into the financial turmoil, how they came out of it, their positioning in the global intellectual capital landscape, and where they can go in the future.

Based on NIC data covering 2005–2010 for 48 countries, the figures and tables presented in this booklet largely reflect situations of the four Southeast Asian countries in the real economy. Malaysia with the highest GDP per capita (ppp) experienced the best NIC ranking gains over the 6 years, whereas the Philippines, with the lowest GDP per capita (ppp), had the largest NIC ranking decline. Data of 48 countries indicate that the higher the NIC, the higher the GDP per capita (ppp), accentuating the value of NIC in major countries throughout the world. *For the 6-year NIC ranking, Malaysia ranked #24, Thailand #34, the Philippines #46, and Indonesia #47.*

The 2008 global financial crisis is considered to be the worst since the Great Depression of the 1930s, with severe impacts being felt all across the globe. This financial crisis came with unexpected speed and spread into a global economic shock, with almost no country being spared. During this period, economies worldwide slowed, credits tightened, and international trade declined. Governments and central banks worldwide responded to the crisis with unprecedented fiscal stimuli, monetary policy expansions, and institutional bailouts in their respective countries. While the financial crisis was declared over by the end of 2009, as of mid-2012, Europe is still mired in the second recession, the U.S. reports only modest growth, even the champion recovery region, Asia, is also experiencing economic slowdown due to the gloomy external environment.

The four Southeast Asian countries were not impacted much by the first wave of the financial crisis triggered by sub-prime mortgages. In fact it was not until global credits tightened, foreign investment rapidly withdrew, and export demands drastically dropped that they were affected. Having weathered the 1997 Asian financial crisis and with their resulting fortified financial systems, these four countries entered into this crisis with relatively strong positions. In addition, each country had good amounts of foreign exchange surplus at the end of 2007 that enabled the governments to provide timely and needed stimulus packages for mitigating the negative impacts of the crisis.

Among the 48 countries, the NIC of Malaysia was in the top 50 %, Thailand in the third quarter percentile, and Indonesia and the Philippines in the last quarter percentile. For short-term NIC, there was a clear decline from 2007 to 2008 in Malaysia and the Philippines, especially in market capital. For long-term NIC, there was a decline from 2007 to 2009 in Indonesia and the Philippines, especially in renewal capital.

The 3D trajectory analysis reveals that *government-related issues are the greatest barricade* to achieving GDP growth. These issues are mainly in the areas of corporate tax encouragement, fair business competition environment, transparency of government policy, government efficiency, and convenience of establishing new firms. When benchmarking Japan's GDP growth, the common areas in which these four Southeast Asian countries need to improve are R&D-related issues, such as patents, R&D % of GDP, and business R&D investment. Based on deficiency scores, Indonesia has the most amount of work to do in order to achieve the targeted GDP, followed by the Philippines, Thailand, and Malaysia.

This economic crisis provides an ideal opportunity for nations to examine the soundness of their economic system and the effectiveness of national governance related to NIC. The following implications are drawn from our research findings. Readers can refer to Chap. 5 for the rationale behind these implications.

1. NIC development goes together with economic development and should be regarded as an enhancer of economic growth.
2. Sound financial systems help withstand external financial shock.
3. Always maintaining adequate amounts of foreign exchange reserves can safeguard a nation from sudden economic shock.
4. Searching for a balance between export encouragement and domestic markets expansion is an important task.
5. Efficient disbursement of assigned stimulus money is even more important than the stimulus plans.
6. Utilizing stimulus packages to launch structural reforms for economic transformation is an effective strategy.
7. Developing renewal capital should generate high value in Malaysia and Thailand.

8. Establishing sound safety nets together with a high growth and export-dependent national development strategy is essential in building a more resilient economy.
9. Pursuing political stability is the formula for a nation's continuous growth.
10. Establishing a regional supporting system is an effective way to combat financial crisis.

The graphs and tables presented in this volume reveal that Malaysia was ranked number one and Thailand number two in both intangibles (NIC) and tangibles (GDP per capita ppp). Indonesia, number four among the four, has the least NIC score fluctuation. Malaysia and Thailand, being more export-dependent, are more susceptible to external impact. Indonesia demonstrates its exceptional economic resilience, with real GDP growth, decreased government debt, and reduced unemployment rate even during and after the financial crisis. This volume also uncovers one important recipe of how these four countries weathered the crisis so well—the ASEAN supporting system. The support system that this group of countries forms together enables them to help each other withstand the external impact without having to rely on the advanced western countries.

In an era when the intangible asset has become a key competitive advantage, investing in NIC development is equivalent to investing in future economic development and well-being. NIC evolution can be nourished both from a local culture viewpoint as well as from a perspective of global interconnectivity via social media.

Based on emerging new insights of values, societal history, and citizen relationships, a key focus for the future will be on the fusion of NIC, social service innovation and societal innovation, for the enabling of a new societal fabric.

Contents

List of Figures

List of Tables

Appendices

Abstract

In the first decade of the new millennium, the biggest event that caught worldwide attention was the 2008 global financial crisis, which was brought about primarily by ineffective governance, failed surveillance systems, and implementation flaws. These problems are mainly intangible in nature. Therefore, examining the financial crisis from the viewpoint of intangible asset provides a different perspective from traditional economic approaches.

National intellectual capital (NIC), mainly consisting of human capital, market capital, process capital, renewal capital, and financial capital, is a valuable intangible asset and a key source of national competitive advantage in today's knowledge economy. This booklet looks into the connections between the 2008 global financial crisis and NIC development with a special focus on Indonesia, Malaysia, The Philippines, and Thailand.

In addition to the summaries of financial crisis impact, the aftermath, future prospects, and challenges of each individual country, NIC analysis based on data covering 2005–2010 for 48 countries reveal that the higher the NIC, the higher the GDP per capita (ppp). Graphical presentations of various types allow for intra-country and inter-country comparisons to position the reported four countries on a world map of NIC–GDP co-development.

By looking into tangible economic development along with intangible NIC development, this booklet provides valuable implications for policymakers.

Keywords Competitiveness · Economic policy · Financial capital · Human capital · Innovation · Intangible assets · Intellectual capital · Knowledge management · Research and development (R&D) · Science and technology policy

Chapter 1
Introduction

In the middle of 2012, the aftermath and lingering effects of the 2008 global financial crisis vary from country to country. Some countries, such as China and India, have recovered and are picking up growth speed, but some countries, such as Spain, are still asking for external financial aid. Even though the Euro zone is still mired in sovereign debt troubles and the global economy has slowed down, the countries to be introduced in this booklet have successfully recovered and are growing. In hindsight, it is valuable to reflect what had happened during the last few years in different countries to gain some insight for future policy implications.

Unexpectedly, what started off as subprime mortgage problems in the financial sector in the U.S. snowballed into the deepest and most widespread financial and economic crisis in the last seven decades. With almost synchronized worldwide recession, global GDP contracted for the first time since World War II according to the international monetary fund (IMF). Governments and central banks around the world have responded to the crisis through both conventional and unconventional fiscal and monetary measures in order to maintain financial order as well as help industries, private companies, and citizens wade through the difficulties.

In 2009, the World Bank estimated that the 2008 global financial crisis would create an additional 53 million people in poverty who live on less than US$2 per day, due to mainly the decline of global economic growth. The magnitude of this crisis is so large that it has disrupted the global financial system and as a result there is no single economy in the world that is completely isolated from the effect of the crisis.

In the wake of the crisis, causes of the disaster have become known, although its impact varies from country to country after combining with local factors. Briefly speaking, the initial collapse of subprime bonds in the U.S. resulted in a shortage in the global money market. As a result, huge amounts of foreign investments were withdrawn from the invested countries all over the world to increase their home companies' liquidity. Thus, the credit squeeze affected domestic market operations. Due to the very negative cash flow position, many companies slashed their production levels and canceled or postponed investment projects (Mendonça 2010). With the tight money market, export demands dropped

C. Y.-Y. Lin et al., *National Intellectual Capital and the Financial Crisis in Indonesia, Malaysia, The Philippines, and Thailand*, SpringerBriefs in Economics,
DOI: 10.1007/978-1-4614-7943-7_1, © The Author(s) 2014

and unemployment increased. Adding to the problem was that some European Union countries were overlending and overspending even before 2008. Consequently, banks in many countries did not have enough money to support the repayment of foreign debts and corporate loans. Thus, confidence fell, which directly hit the consumer market, and a global financial crisis set in.

One key factor that did not guard against the financial crisis was that the conventional financial system failed to detect the potential troubles of subprime bonds largely due to nontransparent information disclosure. Therefore, at the onset of the crisis, management scholars criticized the inability of the traditional accounting system to reveal intangible assets that explain hidden values as well as risks for proper decision making (Reavis 2009). In line with such criticism, intellectual capital (Edvinsson and Malone 1997) advocating the value of human capital, social capital, and so forth, has gained increasing attention in today's keener global competition, which justified the value of examining the connection between national intellectual capital and the 2008 global financial crisis.

It is our deep belief that national intellectual capital, albeit intangible, can provide valuable insights to policy makers regarding future risk control and strategy formulation. Our previous book, *National Intellectual Capital: A Comparison of 40 Countries* (Lin and Edvinsson 2011; www.nic40.org), was born out of this belief and traces the national intellectual capital development of 40 countries over 14 years (1995–2008). The data analysis revealed certain warning signs of impending financial crisis for countries such as Greece, Iceland, and Ireland (Lin and Edvinsson 2011; 327–333). As a followup study, this booklet series is an attempt to further explore the connections between the financial crisis and national intellectual capital development.

The booklet series, in its entirety, will examine the national intellectual capital status of 48 countries from 2005 to 2010, to glean new understanding about whether there is a NIC development pattern that distinguishes countries with fast recovery from those with slow recovery. This is presented through a series of 11 country clusters, with each booklet focusing on one particular cluster. The clusters are determined based upon several factors: geographical proximity, geographical size, or the country's phase of economic development. Focusing on one cluster at a time, we probe the areas of concern within a single country and extend them to compare multiple countries to see whether the situation before and after the crisis can be explained by intangible NIC. Our data come from the well-recognized International Institute for Management Development (IMD) in Switzerland. The IMD has been publishing yearly rankings of World Competitiveness for around two decades. Hopefully, the analysis in this booklet series can provide a different perspective of the financial crisis for future policy decisions.

This volume, Volume Four, will focus on the four Southeast Asian countries: Indonesia, Malaysia, the Philippines, and Thailand. All four countries are the founding members of the ten-country Association of Southeast Asian Nations (ASEAN). ASEAN was established on August 8, 1967 in Bangkok, Thailand to accelerate economic growth, social progress, and cultural development in the region through joint endeavors. Readers can refer to the ASEAN website for the full range of aims and purposes of the association. In 1997, ASEAN invited China, Japan, and Korea to join their 30th year celebration; after that the term "ASEAN+3" was coined.

This booklet first provides an economic background of these four countries as a whole before going into each individual nation's development. Through this process, the author's hope to paint a general picture of the countries' economic conditions and provide a basis for our dataset and analysis in future sections.

Chapter 2 briefly introduces the impact of 2008 financial crisis on the four countries. Chapter 3 elaborates the national intellectual capital development of the four countries. Chapter 4 describes issues beyond the financial crisis and Chap. 5 concludes with future perspective and policy implications.

Economic Background

Since the economic history of the four countries goes back centuries, it is impossible to cover the entire spectrum in our work. As such, this background discussion will consider events in the relative recent history from 2005 onwards that have the most direct impact upon the current economic conditions of each specific country. In addition, particular attention will be given to the 2008 global financial crisis. In doing so, the authors hope that the background, in conjunction with our later data and analysis, will provide a "before, during, and after" picture of what was happening from a macroeconomic and intangible assets viewpoint.

For this country cluster in particular, the 1997 Asian financial crisis merits a brief review as it exerted significant influence on the resilience of these four countries when facing the recent 2008 global financial crisis. The 1997 Asian financial crisis started in Thailand with the financial collapse of the Thai Baht caused by the decision of the Thai Government to float the Baht, cutting its peg to the U.S. dollar on July 2, 1997. According to the US Congressional Research Service Report (1998), after the depreciation of Thai Baht, the Philippines intervened to defend its Peso. Two months later, the Philippine Peso, Malaysian Ringgit, and Indonesian Rupiah continued to fall in addition to Thai Baht. To rescue the countries in trouble, IMF approved an extension of credit to the Philippines of US$1.1 billion and arranged a US$17.2 billion support package for Thailand.

In the wake of the Asian financial crisis, Asian Development Bank conducted research comparing the hardest hit countries with those fared the crisis better and found that financial fundamentals matter a lot (Zhuang and Dowling 2002). Specifically, countries in deep trouble had appreciations in the real exchange rate against both the US dollar and the basket currencies of their major trading partners. Serious problems in the capital account were uncovered, such as the ratio of foreign liabilities to foreign assets of the banking sector. There was also strong evidence of excessive growth of domestic credit, particularly in Malaysia, the Philippines, and Thailand. In addition, evidence showed fast deteriorations in the

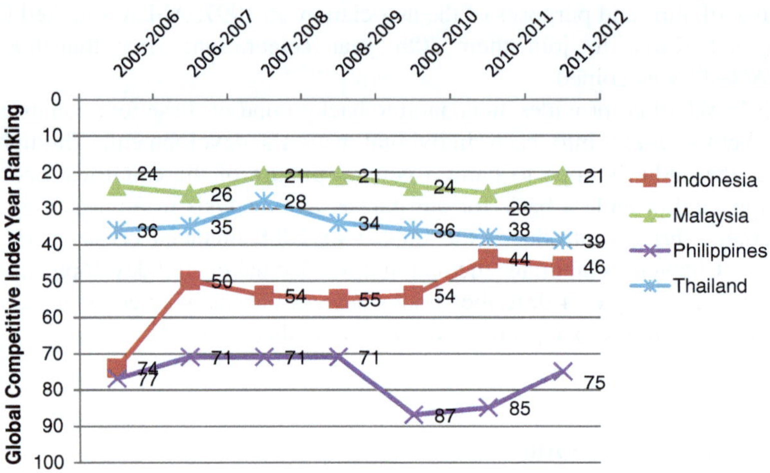

Fig. 1.1 GCI index ranking of the four Southeast Asian countries

real sector and the burst of asset price bubbles, especially in Thailand (Zhuang and Dowling 2002). The painful experience of the Asian financial crisis prompted the four countries to investigate their financial fundamentals and proceeded with required reforms to strengthen their financial system.

In 2012, the 2008 financial crisis is already behind these four countries as their recovery started to show at the last quarter of 2009. To paint a general picture of their global competitiveness in the most recent years and before the financial crisis, we introduce hereunder the Global Competitiveness Index (GCI) published by the World Economic Forum for the reader's reference. This index is relatively robust as it takes into account the 12 distinct pillars[1] containing basic requirements, efficiency enhancers, and innovation factors that contribute to a nation's overall economic strength. Based upon commonly accepted economic theory, the development of 142 countries was split into three stages in which different factors play the dominant role in determining the outcome of a country's economy. Stage 1, Stage 2, and Stage 3 are respectively characterized by being factor, efficiency, and innovation driven (Schwab 2011). Indonesia, Malaysia, and Thailand are categorized as Stage 2 economies, whereas the Philippines progressed from Stage 1 to Stage 2.

Plotting each country's annual ranking against a time series of seven periods, Fig. 1.1 displays a rough pictorial overview of these four countries' global competitiveness before and after the financial crisis. As an indicator of economic strength in 2011–2012, it can be seen that Indonesia #46, Malaysia #21, the

[1] The 12 pillars include: institutions, infrastructure, macroeconomic environment, health and primary education, higher education and training, goods market efficiency, labor market efficiency, financial market development, technological readiness, market size, business sophistication, and innovation.

Philippines #75, and Thailand #39 were ranked in three groups. Malaysia is in the first quarter percentile, Thailand and Indonesia in the second quarter percentile, and the Philippines at the third quarter percentile with a lagging development stage. In other words, Malaysia is relatively strong in global competitiveness in this country cluster.

Over the years, Indonesia had the greatest improvement and its ranking is up from 74 to 46, Malaysia is up from 24 to 21, the Philippines is up from 77 to 75, yet Thailand is down from 36 to 39. From Fig. 1.1, financial crisis seems to have the greatest impact on the Philippines with a drastic ranking decline from 71 to 87 between the two periods of 2008–2009 and 2009–2010. In general, Malaysia and Thailand have less GCI ranking fluctuation over the seven periods.

In September 2011, OECD reported that major economies were tilting back into recession as sovereign debt problems continued to ail the Euro zone (Bryant 2011). Concerns about the fiscal and banking problems continued to weigh on the global economic outlook. In 2011, economic activity contracted further in Europe and the U.S. economy experienced only modest growth.

In January 2012, the World Bank (2012) recommended that developing countries prepare for further downside risks, as Euro Area debt problems and weakening growth in several big emerging economies are dimming global growth prospects. It also lowered its growth forecast for 2012 to 5.4 % for developing countries and 1.4 % for high-income countries (−0.3 % for the Euro Area), down from its earlier estimates of 6.2 and 2.7 % (1.9 % for the Euro Area), respectively. Global growth was projected at 2.5 and 3.1 % for 2012 and 2013, respectively. The World Bank (2012) also predicted that "an escalation of the crisis would spare no-one. Developed- and developing-country growth rates could fall by as much or more than the rates in 2008/2009."

For the Southeast Asian countries, OECD (2011) reported that, as opposed to most OECD economies, the region will enjoy solid growth until 2016. Real GDP is projected to grow at 5.6 % per year on average during 2012–2016 in the six Southeast Asian economies (Indonesia, Malaysia, the Philippines, Singapore, Thailand, and Vietnam), a rate of expansion that is slightly lower than the average of the pre 2008 crisis period (6.1 % for 2003–2007). Specifically, Indonesia is likely to lead the region's growth and will keep the strong momentum with its buoyant domestic demand. Growth prospects in Malaysia, mainly underpinned by its strong investments, will remain robust in the medium term, though slower than the pre 2008 level. The Philippine economy also shows resilience due to its domestic demand and workers' remittances. For Thailand, the unprecedented scale of floods has added to the downside risks in its near-term prospects. For readers' reference, the status of Singapore is reported in Volume Two in this booklet series and Vietnam is not included in this research project due to a lack of data.

Chapter 2 will give a brief background and qualitative analysis of the financial crisis as it relates to these four Southeast Asian countries.

Chapter 2
Impact of the 2008 Global Financial Crisis

The four Southeast Asian countries examined in this study are categorized as emerging economies, each with a sizeable domestic market. At the onset of the 2008 global financial crisis, there was a general belief that they were immune from Western Sub-prime mortgage financial troubles, as their financial sectors had low exposure to the toxic assets and they mainly relied on domestic markets for gross domestic product (GDP) growth. These characteristics should, in theory, make their economies less vulnerable to financial and economic developments in advanced economies (OECD 2010; Ziegenhain 2010). Yet, as the financial crisis continued to roil credit and stock markets around the globe, it turned out that no country was spared the consequences; these four Southeast Asian countries have no exception.

In order to present the impact of the 2008 global financial crisis, this chapter first graphically compares the overall economic development of the four countries during the time period from 2005 to 2010. Then, it elaborates on the impact of the financial crisis on each country individually in the sequence of Indonesia, Malaysia, the Philippines, and Thailand.

The impact of the 2008 global financial crisis on each country can be easily observed from the following four graphs, namely the percentage of real GDP growth per capita, total general government debt percentage of GDP, unemployment rate of labor force, and consumer price inflation (CPI).

Comparisons of the Four Countries

This section presents four graphs in order to examine these four countries as a whole between 2005 and 2010. Figure 2.1 shows that Indonesia has the least real GDP growth decline and fluctuation over the 6 years, sliding from 4.34 % in 2008 to 3.25 % in 2010. The Philippines did not experience negative real GDP growth in 2009 (1.03 %), also its growth rebounded relatively well to 5.30 % in 2010. Malaysia (from 4.87 to −3.14 %) and Thailand (from 4.31 to −3.12 %) had a

C. Y.-Y. Lin et al., *National Intellectual Capital and the Financial Crisis in Indonesia, Malaysia, The Philippines, and Thailand*, SpringerBriefs in Economics,
DOI: 10.1007/978-1-4614-7943-7_2, © The Author(s) 2014

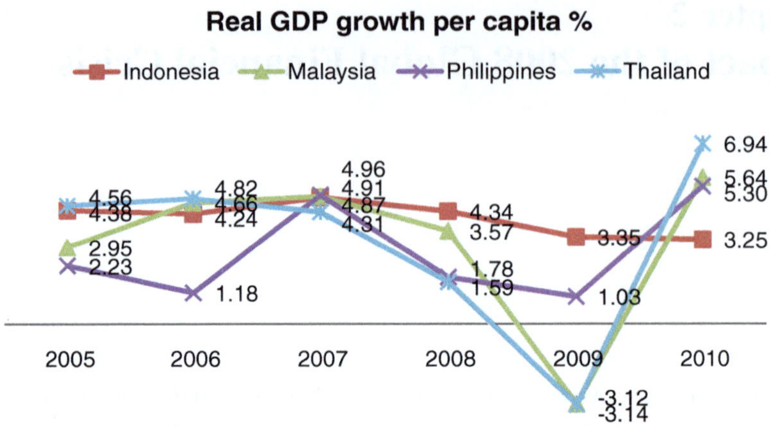

Fig. 2.1 Real GDP growth per capita of Indonesia, Malaysia, the Philippines, and Thailand from 2005–2010

sharper GDP declines from 2007 to 2009. Malaysia and Thailand are the two countries in this country cluster that experienced negative real GDP growth during the financial crisis. Nevertheless, they are also the two countries that experienced strong rebounds of 5.64 and 6.94 % in 2010, respectively. Over the years, the real GDP growth patterns of Malaysia and Thailand were similar. Their sharp decline during the global financial crisis and faster rebound afterwards manifests that these two countries had heavier reliance on exports than the other two countries and were more prone to external impact. Indonesia's strong domestic consumption resulted in its relatively stable real GDP growth even during the financial crisis, which is in concert with OCED's report that Indonesia's 2009 growth is ranked number three in the G20, after China and India.

In terms of the total general government debt as a percentage of the GDP, Fig. 2.2 indicates that Indonesia had a decreasing government debt even during and after the financial crisis. Malaysia and Thailand show similar development patterns with about 20 % point gap in between. Their government debt apparently increased in 2009 reflecting their financial needs. The Philippine Government debt decreased from 2005 to 2007, and then rose a little from 2008 to 2009, yet again decreased in 2010. Comparing to the status of 2005 and 2010, Indonesia and the Philippines saw debt decrease, whereas Malaysia and Thailand saw it increase. From 2009 onwards, Indonesia and Thailand have been in the low debt group (under 30 % of GDP) and Malaysia and the Philippines in the high debt group (over 50 % of GDP).

Reinhart and Rogoff (2009) reported from their research on financial crises over the last 800 years that the aftermath of a financial crisis brings slow and halted growth, sustained high unemployment, and surging public debt—with the overhang of public and private debt being the most important impediment to a normal recovery from the recession.

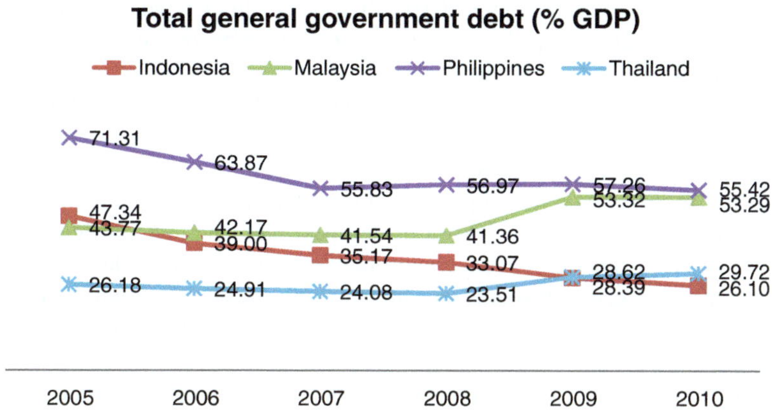

Fig. 2.2 Total General Government Debt (% GDP) of Indonesia, Malaysia, the Philippines, and Thailand from 2005–2010

Figure 2.3 shows that the unemployment rate of Indonesia had a continuous decrease over the 6 years, despite the global financial turmoil. Although its 7.14 % unemployment rate in 2010 is still relatively high, the continuous reduction in unemployment rate is very rare during this global financial crisis. The unemployment rate of the Philippines experienced a sharp decline from 11.5 % in 2005 to 6.30 % in 2007; however it rose a little to 6.80 % in 2008 and increased to over 7 % in 2009 and 2010. The unemployment rate development patterns of Malaysia and Thailand were similar and relatively stable over the 6 years, with Thailand having lower unemployment rate. Both rates increased a little in 2009, yet decreased to lower than their 2005 status in 2010. When comparing the

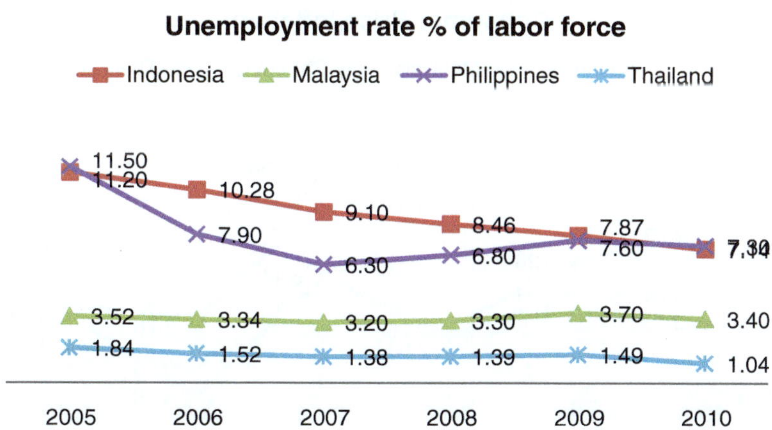

Fig. 2.3 Unemployment rate of Indonesia, Malaysia, the Philippines, and Thailand from 2005–2010

unemployment rate in 2005 and 2010, all four of them have decreases, which manifest that countries in this cluster were not impacted much in terms of unemployment.

Figure 2.4 shows the CPI of the four countries. In this country cluster, Indonesia had the highest inflation and Malaysia the lowest. All the four countries had inflation increase in 2008, afterwards a sharp decrease in 2009, and then bounced back a little in 2010. The development pattern of CPI is somewhat similar for all the four countries, although with various degrees. Thailand had a little deflation in 2009, very likely due to the excess production capacity and depressed global demand during the crisis. It seems that financial crisis did cool down their inflation a little bit. When comparing the CPI between 2005 and 2010, all four countries had a decrease.

In general, the four figures for these four countries indicate that real GDP growth per capita and CPI clearly show the impact of the 2008 global financial crisis. The other two indicators, total general government debt and unemployment rate, are generally going down, which explain that these four countries are resilient to the external economic impact and are recovering. Interestingly, the development patterns of the four indicators of Malaysia and Thailand are pretty similar, showing their comparatively faster economic development as well as their heavier reliance on exports than the other two countries. In general, these four figures indicate that the 2008 financial crisis did exert some impact on their economic development, yet it is not as serious as expected and their recovery is obvious.

In what follows, we briefly describe the impact of the 2008 global financial crisis on these four countries. The depth of the report depends on the English literature available for each economy. For readers to gain a general picture about the efforts that each country has put in mitigating the negative impact of the financial crisis, we have summarized the details of stimulus packages implemented

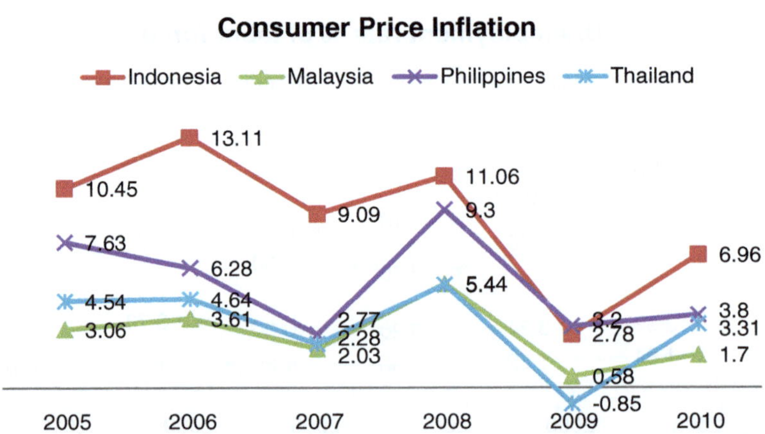

Fig. 2.4 Consumer price inflation of Indonesia, Malaysia, the Philippines, and Thailand from 2005–2010

by these countries in Appendix 1. Please note that the reported package is based on publicly available data and is not an exhaustive list. In addition, the reported amounts of stimulus packages were based on the foreign exchange rate at the time of each stimulus, and thus vary. Readers can also refer to Appendix 2 for the important meetings conducted by key global leaders during this financial crisis.

Indonesia

Indonesia is endowed with the fourth largest population in the world and with abundant and diversified natural resources (OECD 2010). It is now the world's third most populous democracy and home to the world's largest Muslim population (CIA 2012). Indonesia's economy withstood the 2008 global crisis very well (Adriyanto 2009; Boediono 2009; Hill and Manning 2009; and OECD 2010), mainly because of its heavy reliance on domestic consumption, which has contributed a significant share (65 %) of Indonesia's GDP (Titiheruw et al. 2009). In addition, its increased resilience of external economic shocks may stem from substantial macroeconomic and structural reforms undertaken since the Asian crisis (Murniningtyas 2009; OECD 2010). Furthermore, at the end of December 2008, Indonesia had a comfortable amount of international reserves that totaled US$51.6 billion (Bank Indonesia 2009). Based on Indonesia's Central Agency on Statistics, the slowdown of the Indonesian economy started in the third quarter of 2008, worsening in the first and second quarter of 2009, and recovered in the fourth quarter of 2009. OECD (2010) also reports that in 2009, Indonesia's real GDP growth was the third highest in the G20 countries, after China and India.

Although Indonesia's fundamentals in the external sector, fiscal sector, and banking industry were strongly positioned to weather the global crisis (Murniningtyas 2009; Ziegenhain 2010), at the end of 2008, the global financial turbulence still bore down on its economy (Boediono 2009). This crisis affected Indonesia through three channels: First through the stock market, the influence was almost immediate yet not many people were affected; second through a shortage in capital markets, causing an increase in interest rates for deposits and lending; and third through the real sector production, exerting the largest impact (Murniningtyas 2009). For instance, nonoil and gas exports (86.76 % of Indonesia's total exports in January 2009) dropped 30.64 % (year on year) (Titiheruw et al. 2009). In addition, the balance of payments began to accumulate a rising deficit and the exchange rate underwent significant depreciation. In Indonesia's financial markets, global liquidity conditions tightened up in tandem with mounting perceptions of emerging market risks, thus triggering a slide in the Indonesian Stock Market and the downturn of Government Securities prices (Boediono 2009).

As a result, capital outflows accelerated. In addition, global demands dropped sharply. The slowdown in exports brought widespread job losses in the formal economy, with subcontracted, casual and temporary workers in export-oriented industries being the hardest hit. Restricted credit availability for small- and medium-sized enterprises (SMEs) also hampered robust economic rebound and the reabsorption of labor. However, during the last 3 months of 2008 only, there was a 54 % increase (quarter-to-quarter) in assignment of Indonesian workers to overseas destinations (around 258,000 workers, compared with 168,000 recorded at the end of September 2008). The total number of Indonesian workers working abroad as of December 2008 reached 4.4 million workers (Titiheruw et al. 2009), which mitigates the unemployment pressure.

With the sign of recession at the last quarter of 2008, Indonesian Government acted swiftly. In January 2009, the government announced a fiscal stimulus package of US$7.6 billion (Rp73.3 trillion) measuring 1.4 % of GDP (ILO 2010), including a tax and customs stimulus worth US$5.6 billion (Rp56 trillion); and expenditure on infrastructure worth US$1.2 billion (Rp12 trillion) (Murniningtyas 2009). Readers can refer to Appendix 1 for the details of the stimulus package. Actually, even before the passage of the stimulus package, a series of tax reforms and subsidy increases had been implemented by the government in December 2008, including prices reduction for automotive diesel and gasoline (Bank Indonesia 2009; Ziegenhain 2010). In addition, central bank cut its policy rate from 9.5 % in November 2008 to 6.5 % by July 2009 to help businesses and consumers (Heritage 2012). In general, Indonesia's stimulus package had three goals: keep the private consumption growth rate above 4 %, improve the competitiveness and resilience of Indonesian companies, and mitigate the effects of layoffs by means of labor-intensive infrastructure projects (Ziegenhain 2010).

The Indonesian Government strived to overcome the threat of the global crisis by improving market confidence, increasing foreign currency reserve through both bilateral, multilateral financing as well as seeking swap facility from Bank of China and the Bank of Japan. In addition, improving the surveillance of economic activities through the issuance of regulation to limit the import of garments and electronics (among others) was also helpful to mitigate the negative impact of the crisis (Adriyanto 2009). In May 2009, the Asian Development Bank approved a US$1 billion loan to Indonesia in order to assist the country in the wake of the global financial crisis (Ziegenhain 2010). The World Bank's Board of Executive Directors granted a US$2 billion Public Expenditure Support Facility for Indonesia, including a deferred drawdown option in March 2009 (Ziegenhain 2010).

Furthermore, the experience gained in the 1997 crisis led to a higher awareness of macroeconomic risks and to the creation of state-owned regulatory institutions. They include a deposit insurance corporation and a capital market and financial institutions supervisory agency to preside over instruments in monetary and fiscal policy, as well as social programs for lessening the impact on the people's welfare (Murniningtyas 2009; Ziegenhain 2010). Thus, the government was able to react more appropriately to the 2008 economic downturn than would have been the case without this previous experience (Ziegenhain 2010).

Rare in other countries, the Indonesia Government has conducted quantitative and qualitative surveys in three time periods: July/August 2009, October/November 2009, and February/March 2010 to closely monitor the impact of the crisis on the real economy and on the people's welfare (Murniningtyas 2009). Such measures enable the government to control and modify its stimulus implementation to actually meet the people's needs.

Overall, the 2008 global financial crisis did not affect Indonesia as acutely as it did many other countries. The impact was comparatively minimal because Indonesia's macroeconomic preconditions were relatively good, including reduced foreign debt, established financial transaction regulations, and a solid banking sector after the 1997 Asian financial crisis. Its central bank has also been credited to decisive and fast actions at the beginning of this crisis in supporting Indonesian Government's adequate economic stimulus package that favored recovery.

Malaysia

Malaysia, a middle-income country, has transformed itself since the 1970s from a producer of raw materials into an emerging multi-sector economy. Under the current government, Malaysia is attempting to achieve high-income status by 2020 and to move farther up the value-added production chain by attracting investments in high technology industries, biotechnology, and services. The government is also trying to lessen its dependence upon state oil producer Petronas, which supplies more than 40 % of government revenue, and to reduce the economy's dependence on exports by boosting domestic demand (CIA 2012).

Prior to the 2008 financial crisis, the Malaysian central bank maintained healthy financial status and its well-developed regulatory regime had limited Malaysia's exposure to riskier financial instruments and the global financial crisis. According to Bank Negara Malaysia (2009), Malaysian international reserves amounted to US$91.3 billion (RM316.8 billion) as of December 31, 2008 and remained stable at US$91.6 billion (RM317.7 billion) as of February 13, 2009. The level of capitalization of the banking system in Malaysia was at its highest historical level at the onset of the crisis, which was attributed to the efforts that enhanced the credit risk management infrastructure and underwriting practices following the Asian financial crisis (Ibrahim 2010). Nevertheless, Malaysia is still vulnerable to a fall in commodity prices or a general slowdown in global economic activity, because exports are a major component of its GDP.

As an open economy highly integrated with the international market in terms of trade and investment (Mei 2010), Malaysia was eventually hit hard by the global downturn (Ortmans 2011). Its economy experienced the full impact of the global recession in the first quarter of 2009 (Ibrahim 2010). In the first three quarters of 2009, GDP growth had reduced to −6.2, −3.9, and −1.2 %, respectively. The ensuing impact resulted in slowdown in GDP and reduction in exports and imports, in consumption expenditure, and in investment (Mei 2010). The falling exports and contracting GDP had resulted in layoffs, temporary layoffs, and workers facing pay cuts. The worst hit sector was manufacturing (Abidin and Rasiah 2009). Malaysia's trading volume attributable to nonresident participants has been more than 30 % since 2004, the reversal of the portfolio capital flows due to repatriation by foreign participants had affected Malaysian stock market significantly (Mah-Hui and Khoon 2010).

Malaysian Government, in anticipation of a more serious and damaging one with long-term effects than the Asian financial crisis, introduced two rescue packages with attractive fiscal stimuli totaling US$18.1 billion (RM67 billion) or 10.4 % of GDP (Abidin and Rasiah 2009). The purpose of these packages was to absorb retrenchment and the shocks faced by the people because of significantly reduced exports, in addition to accelerate development-related expenditure. An allocation of US$202 million (RM700 million) for training and creating employment opportunities is expected to provide 100,000 training opportunities and job placements through collaboration between the government and private sector (Abidin and Rasiah 2009). In addition, special training and retraining programs for retrenched workers are also offered.

During the 2008 financial crisis, Bank Negara Malaysia supported the easing of monetary policy and introduced comprehensive measures to sustain access to financing, thus mitigated the impact of the heightened risk aversion among banks (Ibrahim 2010). In addition, the concerted and preemptive measures taken by the Bank Negara Malaysia through the accelerated implementation of fiscal stimulus plans contributed to stabilizing the domestic economy in the second quarter and its subsequent recovery in the second half of 2009. As a result, the economy resumed its growth momentum in the fourth quarter of 2009, growing by 4.4 % (Ibrahim 2010).

Uniquely, Malaysian Government did not lose sight of its 2020 goal when planning its stimulus package; therefore, its 2009–2010 budget went further in its attempt to transform Malaysia into a high-income country in the next decade (Abidin and Rasiah 2009).

The Philippines

The Philippines economy was one of the few countries to avoid contraction following the 2008 global financial crisis. The economy weathered the global recession better than its regional peers due to minimal exposure to troubled international securities (Balisacan et al. 2010; CIA; Tiongson 2010), lower dependence on exports, relatively resilient domestic consumption, large remittances from four to five million overseas Filipino workers, and a growing business process outsourcing industry (CIA 2012). The Philippine stock market was actually one of the least affected by the global financial crisis in the Asia–Pacific region (Yap et al. 2009). In the past two decades, domestic consumption has been the main driver of the Philippine economy and personal consumption expenditure has contributed about three-fourths of the GDP growth in recent years (Balisacan et al. 2010). The fairly sound fundamentals of its domestic financial sector since the Asian financial crisis in 1997 also made the Philippines less vulnerable to the external shock (Balisacan et al. 2010; Yap et al. 2009). Its gross international reserves which reached US$37.55 billion as of end-December 2008 was 11.3 % higher than the previous year's level of US$33.75 billion (Bangko Sentral ng Philipinas 2009: 29). The Philippine foreign exchange reserves maintained an upward trend despite the fall in exports and larger capital outflows (Yap et al. 2009).

While financial markets in emerging Asian economies had relatively limited exposure to subprime-related instruments, increased global market integration meant that the deleveraging process in advanced economies led to a substantial liquidation of assets in emerging Asian markets and large capital outflows (Guinigundo, n.d.). As a result, the Philippines was not spared the fallout from the crisis, as its GDP growth decelerated considerably in the fourth quarter of 2008 and first half of 2009 (Yap et al. 2009). The Philippines was affected by the crisis in three aspects: exports, remittances from overseas Filipino workers, and foreign direct investments. Private sector flows declined, which led to a net outflow of US$708 million in 2009, a sharp contrast with a net inflow of US$507 million in 2008 (Yap et al. 2009).

Another hidden impact is that although the U.S. accounts for only 18 % of total Philippine exports, a large share of Philippine exports to Japan, China, Hong Kong, South Korea, Taiwan, and Malaysia, which take up another 50 % of exports, were in fact intermediate components of final products bound for the U.S. and European countries (Tiongson 2010). Consequently, the Philippines was indirectly hit by reduced global demands. On the production side, significant slowdowns occurred in manufacturing, electricity, gas and water, trade, and finance services (Yap et al. 2009). In the first quarter of 2009, cumulative net FDI flows fell by over 80 % compared to the same quarter during the previous year, reflecting negative investor sentiment worldwide and the global credit crunch (Tiongson 2010).

To stimulate the economy through the Department of Finance and National Economic and Development Authority (NEDA), the Philippine Government crafted a US$7 billion (PhP330 billion) Economic Resiliency Plan (ERP) which amounted to a total of 4 % GDP (Balisacan et al. 2010; Yap et al. 2009). The ERP was geared toward stimulating the economy through a mix of government spending, tax cuts, and public–private partnership projects. Specifically, it involved essentially front loading the spending of the 2009 government budget and increased spending on responses to the crisis, including cash transfers, food subsidies, tax exemptions (for those earning minimum wage and below), and emergency job creation. In addition, repair and rehabilitation of roads, hospitals, bridges and irrigation facilities, school, and government buildings were also on the agenda (Balisacan et al. 2010; Yap et al. 2009). Consequently, government spending (as a proportion of GDP) in 2009 was 2.8 % points higher than its long-term trend (Balisacan et al. 2010).

Surprisingly, in spite of the sharp changes in trade and investment, the national unemployment rate increased only slightly to 7.5 % at the end of 2009 from 7.4 % a year earlier (Tiongson 2010), with a whole year unemployment rate posted at 6.80 % in 2008 and 7.60 % in 2009 (Fig. 2.4). Very likely, a more stable global environment has led to the resurgence in foreign portfolio equity investment into emerging markets (Yap et al. 2009). Net inflows gradually recovered, and by

October 2009, total net inflows had reached US$1.3 billion dollars; up from US$1.1 billion dollars over the same period in 2008 (Tiongson 2010). In addition, remittances from overseas Filipinos in 2008 alone amounted to $16.4 billion or 13 % of the GDP (Yap et al. 2009). Despite the challenging global economic environment, the Philippines has made a notable recovery since mid 2009, driven mainly by strong export performance (Heritage 2012).

Yet hidden by these positive statistics, ironically, the relative resilience of the Philippine economy can be partly attributed to limited economic expansion during the past three to four decades (Yap et al. 2009). Also, like many other emerging markets, the slowdown was not primarily a result of the global financial crisis. Rather, the deceleration in the Philippine economy was largely brought about by a surge in inflation triggered by the sharp rise of food and fuel prices (Yap et al. 2009). During the 2008 financial crisis, nearly two million Filipinos were pushed to poverty (Balisacan et al. 2010: 33).

Thailand

With a well-developed infrastructure, a free enterprise economy, pro-investment policies, and strong export industries, Thailand enjoyed solid growth from 2000 to 2007, averaging more than 4 % per year, as it recovered from the Asian financial crisis of 1997 (CIA 2012). During the 2008 global financial crisis, although Thailand was not close to the epicenter of the crisis, it was also affected, though less by the turmoil in the U.S. and European financial sectors, but more with the subsequent global slowdown. Since the last quarter of 2008, the slowing external demand adversely affected the Thai economy in terms of tumbling exports, reducing growth, and rising unemployment (Chirathivat and Mallikamas 2010). Thailand's past economic expansion resulted in the country becoming more dependent on its external sector. By 2008, its size of trade was growing at a level 1.3 times the size of its GDP, particularly with the export dependence passing from 46.5 % in 1997 to 72.9 % in 2008 (Chirathivat and Mallikamas 2010). Particularly, the troubled G-3 (the U.S., Japan and EU) markets' share represents around half of Thailand's total exports in 2000 (Chirathivat and Mallikamas 2010).

Thailand's financial and stock markets were already hit in the second half of 2008 that directly resulted from companies' cash flow repositioning and the outflows of funds back to the U.S. and Europe (Chirathivat and Mallikamas 2010). Thai stock market lost about half of its value at the end of 2008 (Kritayanavaj 2008). Fortunately, Thai banks' foreign investments were less than 2 % of their total asset with investment in foreign debt instruments being around 13 % of total debt instrument holdings. Foreign banks account for about 12 % of the Thai market and nonperforming loans have been declining and stood at 3.3 % of total loans in the third quarter of 2008, compared to 4.4 % in same quarter of 2007 (Verghis and Bhaopichitr 2008). These characteristics somewhat insulated Thai economy from the global financial turmoil.

However, the major shock wave began with the impact to the real economy, such that the country's exports were continuously reducing at an average rate of around 20 % monthly from November 2008 up to July 2009, with most sectors experiencing double-digit decreases (Chirathivat and Mallikamas 2010; CIA 2012). For the manufacturing production, the capacity utilization of the sector had particularly been affected for the first and second quarter of 2009 and unemployment reached its highest level in January 2009, with a total of 900,000 unemployed persons (Chirathivat and Mallikamas 2010). In 2009, the economy contracted 2.2 % (CIA 2012).

The tourism industry was severely affected, not only from external economic decline but also from domestic political instability (Kritayanavaj 2008). Tourist arrivals at Bangkok international airport fell by 16 % in the third quarter of 2008, caused by continued political unrest and the slowdown in the global economy (Verghis and Bhaopichitr 2008). Private investments and domestic consumption were affected by political instability and the worsening economy, resulting in lower sentiment, and consumer confidence (Kritayanavaj 2008).

In January 2009, Thailand's new government announced its stimulus package right after taking control of the administration. Its first stimulus package of US$3.27 billion (Bt115 billion) was designed to increase the domestic demand as soon as possible, to alleviate the domestic producers due to the collapse of the external demand, and partly to prevent job losses from a sharp adjustment in production decrease in different industries (Chirathivat and Mallikamas 2010). An additional package of US$ 1.42 billion (Bt50 billion) soon followed with a particular focus on tax measures. The packages consisted of three components: spending, tax reduction measures, and financial measures, including income transfers, subsidies for utilities and transport, and public investment. Readers can refer to Appendix 1 for the details of Thailand's stimulus packages.

In addition, as a quasi-fiscal policy to revitalize the economy and develop infrastructure, the Thai Government planned for a loan of US$22 billion (Bt200 billion) from local banks and US$7.7 billion (Bt70 billion) from the World Bank, Asian Development Bank, and *Japan International Cooperation Agency*. The domestic borrowing of US$22 billion was used to increase the liquidity of state enterprises and the foreign borrowing of US$7.7 billion was used to raise the equity of government banks and support urgent infrastructure development projects. With higher capital, government banks could provide more loan and credit guarantees for farmers, exporters, importers, and SMEs, who face a sharp decline in loan from private banks (Chirathivat and Mallikamas 2010). The money was also for "hard" infrastructure, mainly improving transport and logistics, such as roads, rails, and irrigation projects (Chirathivat and Mallikamas 2010).

Since the Thai economic fundamentals remain relatively solid, once the investors' confidence came back, the economy moved forward fast. With the support of a relatively large international reserve of US$111 billion in 2008 (Chirathivat and Mallikamas 2010; Exim Bank 2009) and the stimulus packages, the Bank of Thailand successfully managed and limited the volatility of Thai currency. Signs of recovery began to show in the last quarter of 2009 (Chirathivat and Mallikamas 2010). As the Thai economy rebounded quickly from the economic slowdown, household consumption, private investment, and exports continued to improve as a result of government economic stimulus programs and global economic recovery. Confidence of foreign travelers into Thailand also returned after the domestic political conflict was eased (Chirathivat and Mallikamas 2010). In general, the economy in Thailand improved slightly from the third quarter and returned to a satisfactory recovery in the last quarter of 2009, of course with some differences among different sectors (Chirathivat and Mallikamas 2010).

Chapter 3
National Intellectual Capital Development of the Four Southeast Asian Countries

In this chapter, we first present the development of national intellectual capital in the four countries over 6 years, and then graphically display the relationship between each individual component of NIC with GDP per capita (ppp). Afterward, we describe the relative positions of long-term and short-term intellectual capital in these four countries and explain the dynamics of NIC for three time periods (2005–2006, 2007–2008, and 2009–2010). Finally, we illustrate the NIC trajectory of these four countries on three dimensional (3D) 48-country landscapes.

National Intellectual Capital Development

The NIC measurement model in this study is based upon the indicators described in Appendix 3, which contains human capital, market capital, process capital, renewal capital, and financial capital. This model has been statistically proven for its validity and reliability. The definitions of the indicators are listed in Appendix 4. This booklet series covers a total of 48 countries in 11 country clusters (see Appendix 5 for details).

For a full picture of all 48 countries, Appendix 6 exhibits the scores and rankings of human capital, market capital, process capital, renewal capital, financial capital, and overall NIC covered in this booklet series. Table 3.1 summarizes the status of these four countries compared with the 48 countries reported in Appendix 6. Appendix 7 provides the individual economic profiles with additional statistics. Appendix 8 reports fiscal stimulus statistics for selected ASEAN countries.

For the 6-year NIC ranking, Malaysia ranked 24, followed by Thailand at 34, the Philippines at 46, and Indonesia at 47. From Table 3.1, it can be seen that Malaysia particularly excels in market capital (rank #9).

The following six figures compare human capital, market capital, process capital, renewal capital, financial capital, and NIC for the four countries. All individual capital scores are based on a 1–10 scale with the NIC score being the sum of the five capital scores.

C. Y.-Y. Lin et al., *National Intellectual Capital and the Financial Crisis in Indonesia, Malaysia, The Philippines, and Thailand*, SpringerBriefs in Economics, DOI: 10.1007/978-1-4614-7943-7_3,

Table 3.1 National intellectual capital ranking of Indonesia, Malaysia, the Philippines, and Thailand (2005–2010)

Country	Human capital		Market capital		Process capital		Renewal capital		Financial capital		NIC	
	Score	Ranking	Score	Ranking	Score	Ranking	Score	Ranking	Score	Ranking	Score	Ranking
Indonesia	4.062	47	4.832	33	3.257	44	1.519	42	7.594	46	21.263	47
Malaysia	6.538	26	6.410	9	5.567	23	2.186	31	8.740	35	29.442	24
Philippines	4.772	43	4.464	40	3.317	43	1.268	47	7.481	47	21.302	46
Thailand	5.310	38	5.524	22	4.365	33	1.436	43	8.304	43	24.938	34

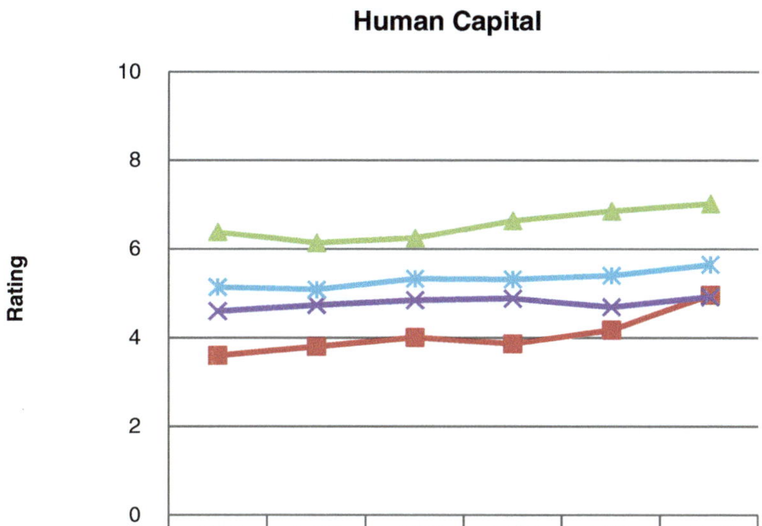

	2005	2006	2007	2008	2009	2010
Indonesia	3.59	3.80	4.00	3.85	4.17	4.95
Malaysia	6.37	6.13	6.24	6.63	6.85	7.01
Philippines	4.59	4.73	4.84	4.88	4.68	4.91
Thailand	5.13	5.08	5.32	5.31	5.39	5.64

Fig. 3.1 Human capital of Indonesia, Malaysia, the Philippines, and Thailand

Human Capital

National human capital represents a nation's investment in nurturing qualified human resources, such as higher education enrollment, skilled labor, and public expenditure in education. Human capital is a long-term oriented NIC (Lin and Edvinsson 2011: 323). As such, it takes time to develop and is not susceptible to external impact. Figure 3.1 shows that the human capital scores of these four countries increased over the 6 years studied. Malaysia consistently had the highest score, followed by Thailand. Indonesia caught up with the Philippines in 2010. Among the four countries, Indonesia and Malaysia have relatively larger scale human capital improvements than the other two countries.

Market Capital

National market capital mainly refers to the general assets embodied in a nation's relationship with the international market, such as cross-border ventures, globalization, and exports of goods. Figure 3.2 shows that most countries have market

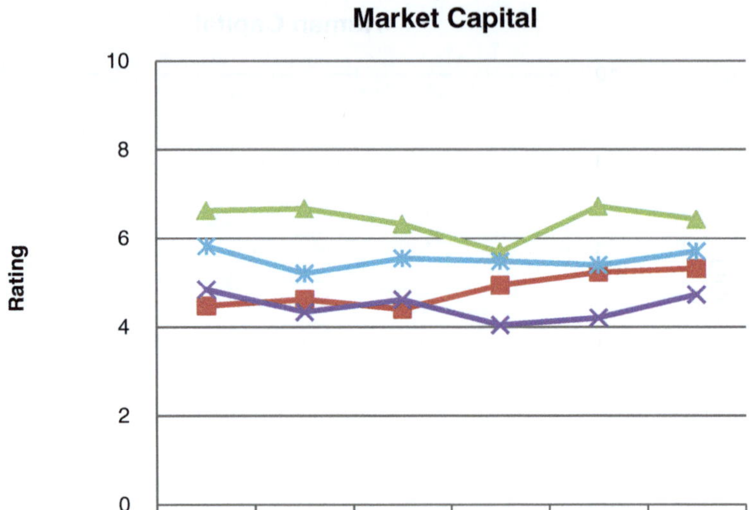

	2005	2006	2007	2008	2009	2010
Indonesia	4.48	4.62	4.40	4.94	5.23	5.32
Malaysia	6.63	6.67	6.32	5.69	6.72	6.43
Philippines	4.84	4.34	4.62	4.05	4.21	4.73
Thailand	5.82	5.21	5.54	5.48	5.39	5.70

Fig. 3.2 Market capital of Indonesia, Malaysia, the Philippines, and Thailand

capital decrease comparing the scores of 2005 and 2010, except Indonesia. Rare globally, Indonesia had a continuous market capital increase starting 2008. Having the lowest market capital score in 2005, Indonesia surpassed the Philippines in 2008. Scores of Malaysia and the Philippines showed a clear dip in 2008, exhibiting the impact of 2008 financial crisis. However, both recovered rapidly showing rebounds in the following year. Thailand had the most stable market capital over the 6 years among the four countries.

Process Capital

National process capital represents the infrastructure required for building a prosperous society, such as capital availability, mobile phone subscribers, and government efficiency. Figure 3.3 shows that process capital of Indonesia and the Philippines are very close to each other starting from 2006. Malaysia consistently had the highest score with a little decline in 2008 and a strong rebound in 2009, showing its good recovery from the financial crisis. Thailand, being the second highest score country, had process capital increase in 2008, yet a delayed decline

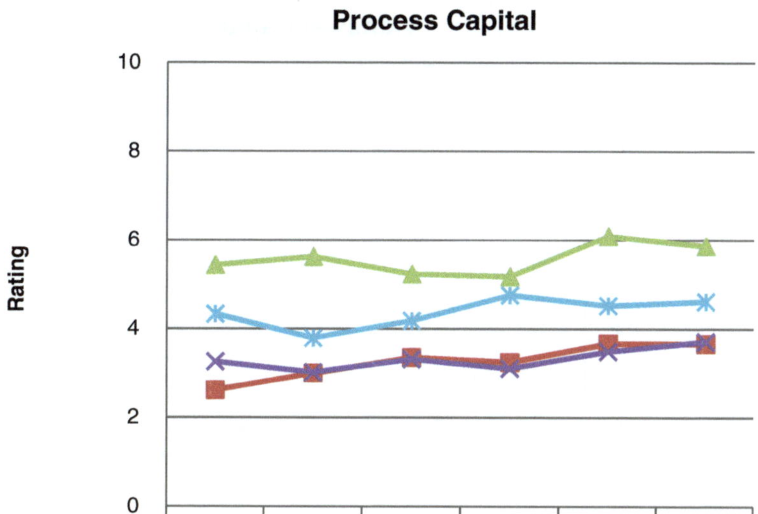

	2005	2006	2007	2008	2009	2010
Indonesia	2.62	3.00	3.35	3.25	3.67	3.67
Malaysia	5.43	5.62	5.23	5.17	6.09	5.86
Philippines	3.26	3.02	3.32	3.11	3.49	3.71
Thailand	4.33	3.79	4.18	4.75	4.52	4.62

Fig. 3.3 Process capital of Indonesia, Malaysia, the Philippines, and Thailand

in 2009. When comparing the scores of 2005 and 2010, all four countries had upward trend with the same relative position. Indonesia and the Philippines had a similar development starting from 2006.

Renewal Capital

National renewal capital represents a country's capability for R&D and innovation in areas such as R&D spending, scientific articles, and patents. Figure 3.4 shows that Indonesia had the same renewal capital score in 2005 and 2010, however, with more ups and downs than the other three countries over the years. Malaysia consistently had the highest score with a little score increase over the years. The Philippines and Thailand had a little decline, yet with relatively stable development over the years. Interestingly, Indonesia had a big score jump in 2007, yet declined to its 2005 position in 2010. Renewal capitals of Indonesia, the Philippines, and Thailand were all at a relatively low level, ranked 42, 47, and 43, respectively, out of 48 countries (Table 3.1).

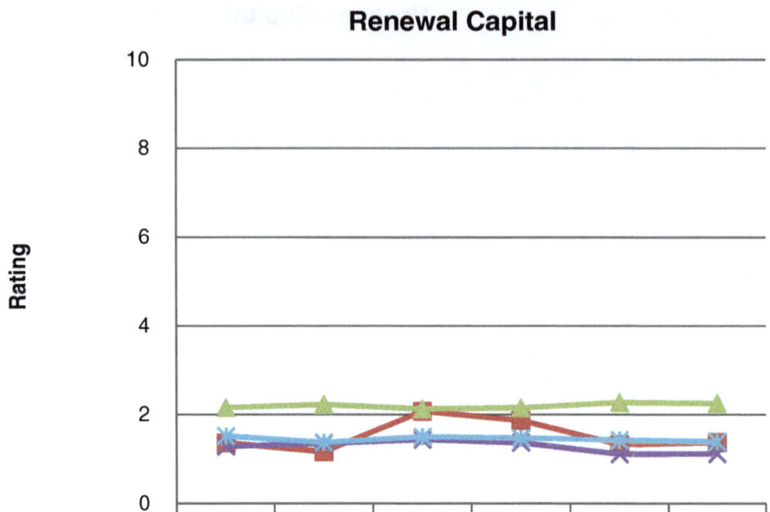

	2005	2006	2007	2008	2009	2010
Indonesia	1.36	1.15	2.06	1.86	1.32	1.36
Malaysia	2.15	2.22	2.11	2.14	2.26	2.24
Philippines	1.27	1.34	1.42	1.36	1.10	1.11
Thailand	1.51	1.36	1.49	1.46	1.41	1.38

Fig. 3.4 Renewal capital of Indonesia, Malaysia, the Philippines, and Thailand

Financial Capital

Financial capital is representative of a country's GDP per capita (ppp) in US dollars transformed to a score on a scale of 1–10. The process of score transformation is explained in detail in Appendix 3. Figure 3.5 shows that the four countries do not have much 1–10 scale financial capital difference. However, consistently, Malaysia had the highest score, followed by Thailand, Indonesia, and the Philippines. In real dollars, the average GDP per capita (ppp) of 2005–2010 is US$3,820 for Indonesia, US$13,226 for Malaysia, US$3,369 for the Philippines, and US$8,236 for Thailand.

NIC

NIC is the overall national intellectual capital comprising of the five types of capital described in the sections above. Figure 3.6 presents the trends of overall NIC over the years. Again, Malaysia consistently had the highest score, followed by Thailand. Indonesia had a continuous NIC improvement over the years,

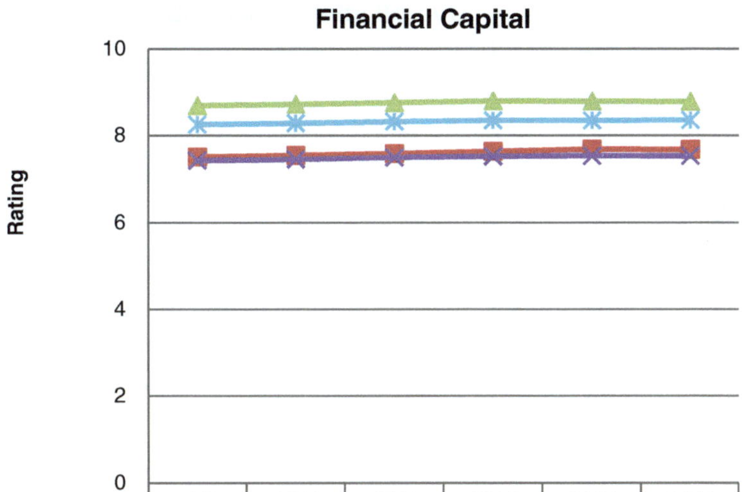

	2005	2006	2007	2008	2009	2010
Indonesia	7.50	7.53	7.57	7.62	7.67	7.67
Malaysia	8.67	8.71	8.74	8.78	8.77	8.77
Philippines	7.41	7.44	7.48	7.51	7.52	7.52
Thailand	8.24	8.27	8.31	8.33	8.33	8.34

Fig. 3.5 Financial capital of Indonesia, Malaysia, the Philippines, and Thailand

surpassing the Philippines in 2008. All four countries had slight overall intellectual capital increase over the years, with Malaysia and Thailand sliding a little in 2008 and in 2009. Malaysia had a relatively large-scale NIC increase in 2009; however, Indonesia had the largest NIC progress over 6 years, demonstrating its future potential in terms of national intangible assets.

The Relationship Between Each Individual Capital and GDP Per Capita (ppp)

We investigate the relationship between each individual capital and economic growth by using six figures (Figs. 3.7–3.12). The graphs have four dimensions: the X axis varies from graph to graph (NIC, human capital, market capital, process capital, and renewal capital), the Y axis is a fixed dimension of GDP per capita (ppp) in US dollars (hereafter termed GDP), the color shade represents renewal capital with red denoting higher levels of renewal capital, and the bubble size denotes the population of a country. Figure 3.7 is the relationship between NIC and GDP for all 48 countries. Figures 3.8, 3.9, 3.10, 3.11, 3.12 display the

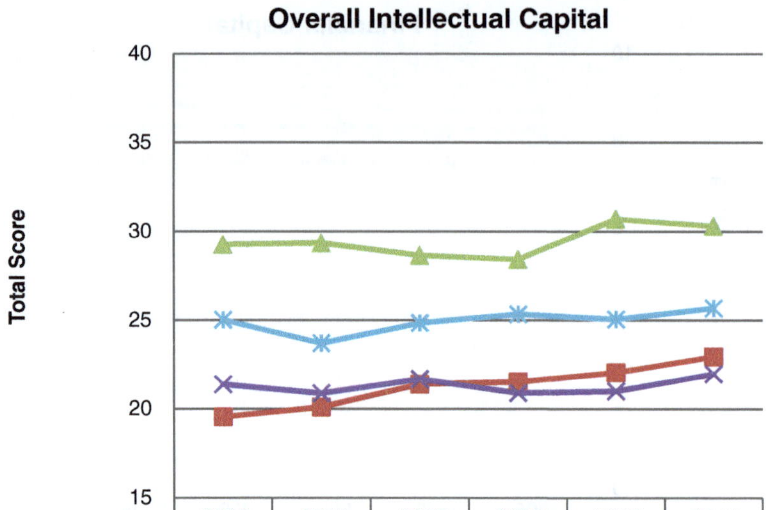

	2005	2006	2007	2008	2009	2010
Indonesia	19.54	20.10	21.39	21.52	22.06	22.97
Malaysia	29.25	29.34	28.64	28.42	30.69	30.31
Philippines	21.38	20.87	21.68	20.89	21.00	21.98
Thailand	25.02	23.71	24.84	25.33	25.05	25.68

Fig. 3.6 Overall intellectual capital of Indonesia, Malaysia, the Philippines, and Thailand

co-development of the intellectual capital-GDP relationship over the 6-year timeframe for the four countries. Since financial capital is the transformed 1–10 score from GDP, there is no need to plot its relationship against itself. In the figures, 2005 is the starting point tagged with the name of the country, and the end point is 2010.

In particular, Fig. 3.7 is plotted to clearly show a full picture of the relationship between NIC and GDP for 48 countries in year 2010. The strong positive correlation indicates that the higher the NIC the higher the GDP. Consequently, it can be seen that enhancing NIC is definitely a strategic issue that deserves the attention of national policy makers.

With the data of all 48 countries, Fig. 3.8 shows the formation of the NIC and GDP co-development continuum from the bottom left to the upper right. The paths of these four countries are located at the bottom end of the continuum, except for Malaysia in the middle right. Thailand's path is in between the four countries, and Indonesia and the Philippines are overlapping in their development. All four countries show a relatively flat or horizontal movement tilted toward the X axis of NIC rather than the Y axis of GDP. In other words, their GDP did not grow much compared to their NIC over the 6 years. However, most of their NIC improved after the financial crisis based on the path development.

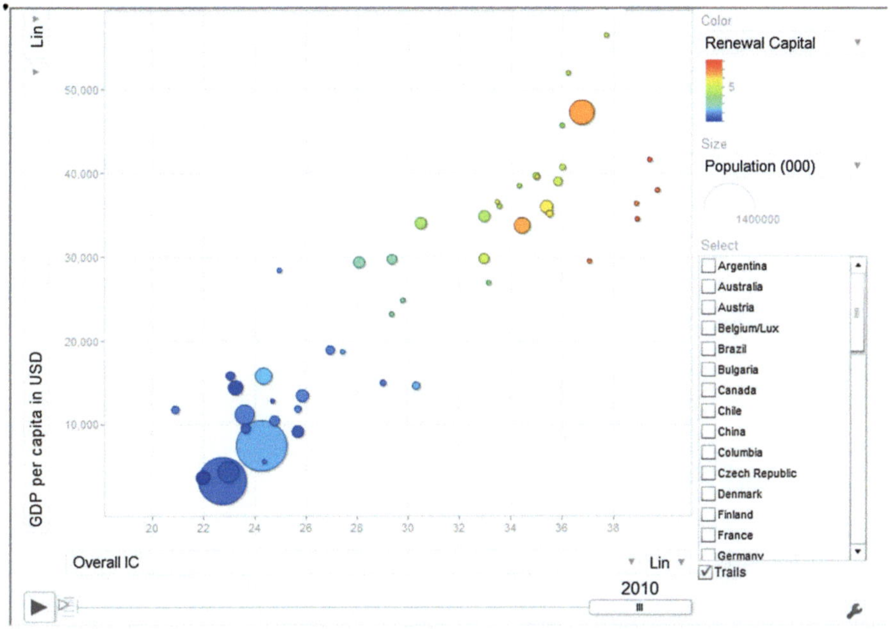

Fig. 3.7 Overall intellectual capital versus GDP per capita (ppp) for 48 countries in 2010

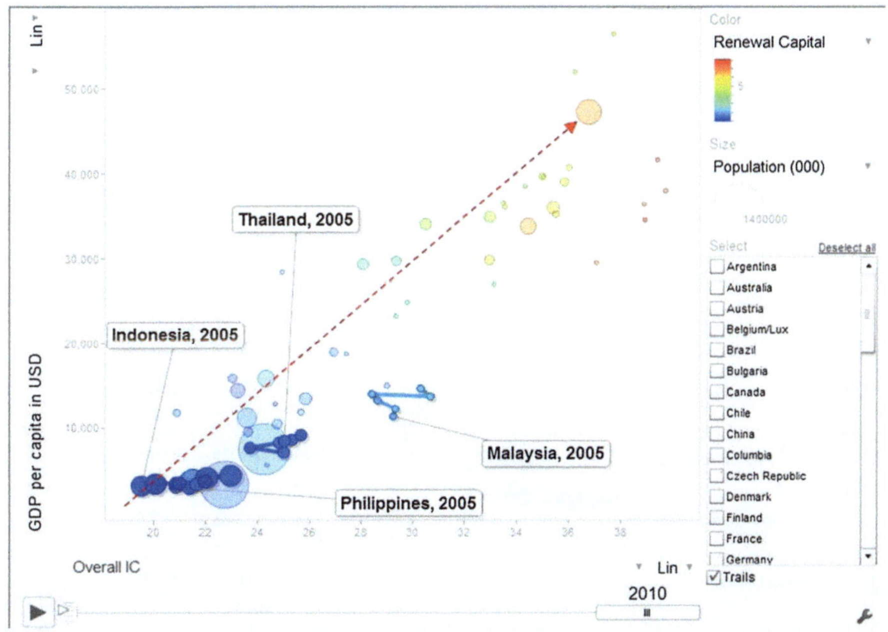

Fig. 3.8 The development of NIC and GDP per capita (ppp) for Indonesia, Malaysia, the Philippines, and Thailand from 2005 to 2010

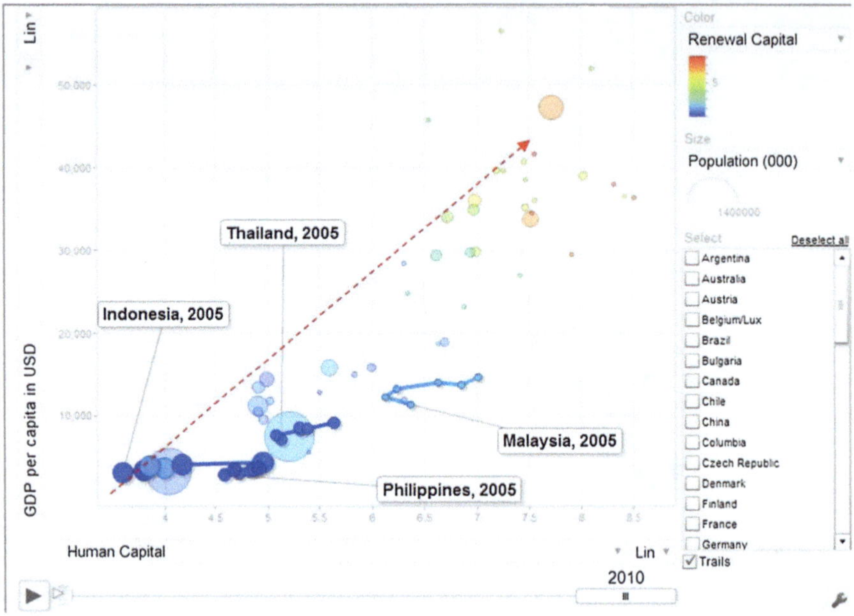

Fig. 3.9 The development of human capital and GDP per capita (ppp) for Indonesia, Malaysia, the Philippines, and Thailand from 2005 to 2010

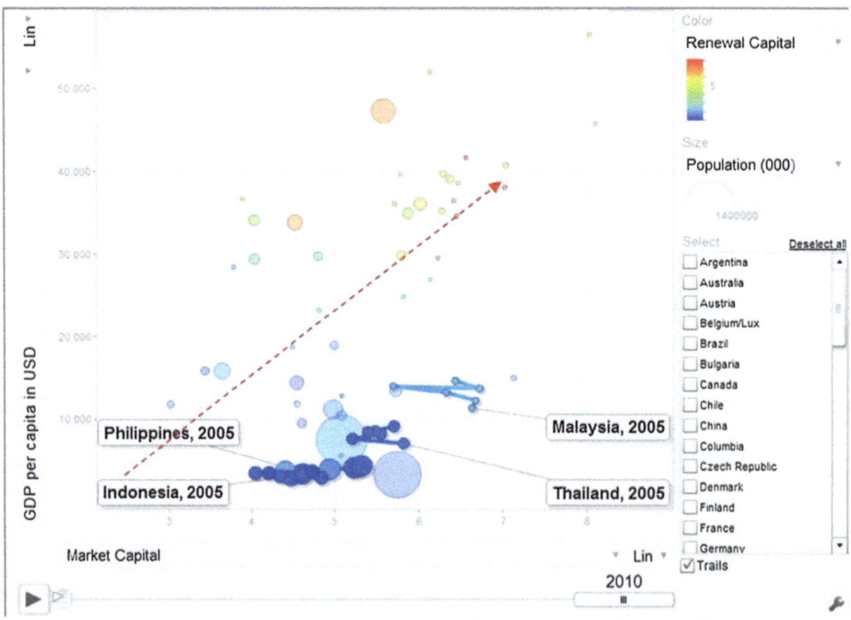

Fig. 3.10 The development of market capital and GDP per capita (ppp) for Indonesia, Malaysia, the Philippines, and Thailand from 2005 to 2010

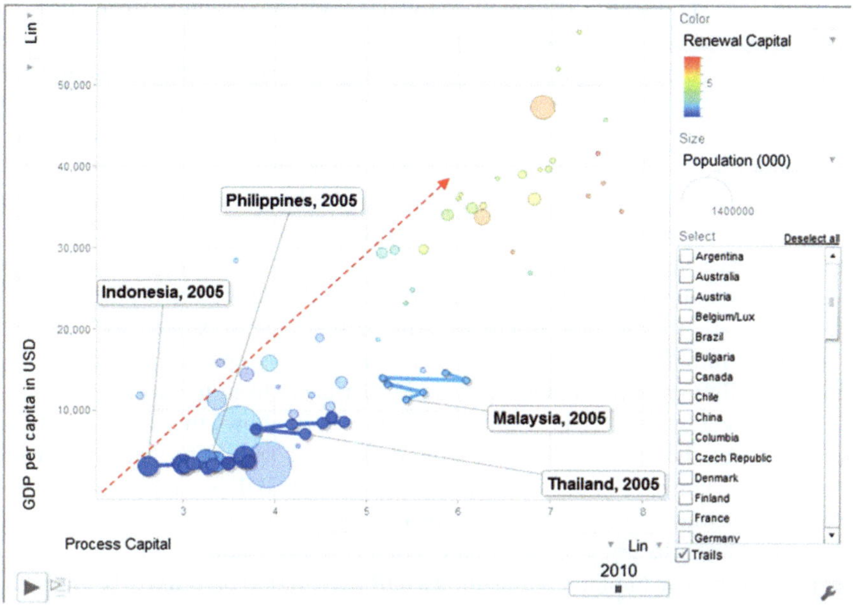

Fig. 3.11 The development of process capital and GDP per capita (ppp) for Indonesia, Malaysia, the Philippines, and Thailand from 2005 to 2010

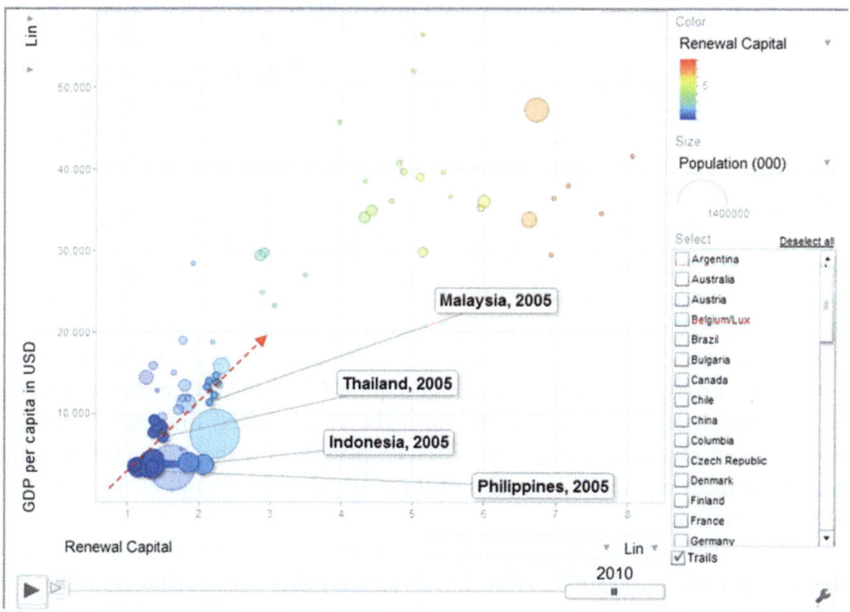

Fig. 3.12 The development of renewal capital and GDP per capita (ppp) for Indonesia, Malaysia, the Philippines, and Thailand from 2005 to 2010

Figure 3.9 shows the "human capital–GDP" continuum formation for 48 countries and the co-development paths of the four countries. Again the development paths of these countries are located at the bottom end of the continuum, with Malaysia standing out in the middle of the continuum. Figure 3.9 is somewhat similar to Fig. 3.8, with Malaysia exhibiting higher human capital than the other three countries, Thailand is in between the four countries, and Indonesia and the Philippines are overlapping in development. Yet, Indonesia had greater human capital improvement than the Philippines over the 6 years. The co-developments of human capital and GDP of these four countries are also relatively flat. However, Malaysia's development path is farther away from the dotted line to the right than Fig. 3.8. Apparently Malaysia has much better human capital, ranked 26 (Table 3.1) compared to the 38–47 ranking range of its neighboring countries. Yet, its correlation with GDP growth is tenuous, being farther away from the dotted line.

The "market capital-GDP" formation of Fig. 3.10 shows that there is no clear continuum like the last two figures as the data points spread further apart, which means that the correlation between market capital and GDP is not high for these 48 countries as a whole. It also shows that market capital of advanced countries is not necessarily better than that of developing countries. For example, market capital of the U.S. (the bigger bubble approaching GDP US$50,000 at Y axis) is lower than that of India (the right big bubble at the bottom center of the graph).

Figure 3.10 shows that the co-development of market capital and GDP in this country cluster gathered at the right hand side of the dotted line, mainly with horizontal movements without much GDP progress over the years.

From Chap. 2, it is clear that the economies of these four countries are gradually integrating with the world economy through expanding international trade. However, with the exception of Indonesia, their market capital scores in 2010 are still lower than in 2005 (Fig. 3.2). As described earlier, market capital is the area in which developing countries can outperform advanced countries with relatively quick results. Therefore, countries in this cluster can strategize toward this area to regain strength.

Figure 3.11 shows that the belt-shaped continuum appears again. This figure is similar to that of Fig. 3.9, with Malaysia having higher process capital than the other three countries, Thailand in the middle, and Indonesia and the Philippines with overlapping paths. Process capital scores for all four countries are higher in 2010 than in 2005, reflecting the results of their infrastructure investments during the financial crisis. Again, their process capital-GDP co-development paths are relatively flat. Malaysia is still at the far right of the dotted line, representing its process capital improved more than its GDP growth over the years. Interestingly, positions of most of the 48 countries at the background also fall at the right hand side of the dotted line.

Figure 3.12 shows that there is no clear continuum for the 48 countries with a different renewal capital and GDP co-development pattern of the four countries from the previous ones. Their development paths were crowded at the left bottom corner of the graph. Even though the development was in a very small scale, the correlation between renewal capital and GDP is higher for Malaysia and Thailand than the other two countries. The phenomenon implies that Malaysia and Thailand can pay more attention to renewal capital improvement for potential GDP growth. The paths of Indonesia and the Philippines are flat and overlapping, indicating their renewal capital progress or regression was not accompanied with GDP growth.

In summary, the above six figures convey certain messages. First, Malaysia is ahead of the other three countries in every type of capital and shows a good recovery after the financial crisis from a NIC perspective. Second, renewal capitals for Malaysia and Thailand have higher correlations with their GDP growth than the other two countries. Third, most of the co-development paths presented above are relatively flat for all the countries, indicating NIC improvement did not accompany good GDP growth. Fourth, generally the development paths of Malaysia are farther away from the dotted line, revealing that the added value of NIC in Malaysia needs to be carefully examined. Fifth, although Indonesia and the Philippines had overlapping development over the 6 years, Indonesia advanced better than the Philippines.

Long-Term and Short-Term National Intellectual Capital

In addition to the six figures in the previous section that show the relationship of each individual capital with GDP, Figs. 3.13 and 3.14 further plot the relationships between human capital and renewal capital, as well as the relationship between market capital and process capital. In our first study (Lin and Edvinsson 2011: 324), we found that the combined increase in human capital and renewal capital led to a nation's long-term development; whereas the combined increase in market capital and process capital might result in more immediate economic development. To present their relationships, Figs. 3.13 and 3.14 map the four capitals on a coordinate with two types of presentation. Based on the same dataset, Figs. 3.13a and 3.14a exhibit a scatterplot for the four countries only, whereas Figs. 3.13b and 3.14b show all 48 countries in the background so that readers will know the relative positions of these four countries. Please note that the connotation of color shade for Figs. 3.13 and 3.14 has been changed from renewal capital to GDP per capita (ppp).

In terms of long-term NIC, both Fig. 3.13a and b indicate that Malaysia is first, followed by Thailand, the Philippines, and Indonesia in that sequence. Figure 3.13a shows that renewal capitals of all four countries are within the range of 1.0 and 2.4; whereas human capitals are within the range of 3.5 and 7.0. In other words, their human capital is much higher than renewal capital. Since renewal capital advancement relies on good quality human capital, countries aspiring to build long-term intangible assets can plan for utilizing human capital to improve renewal capital. When modeling the well-performing countries as shown at the upper right corner of Fig. 3.13b, it is clear that they excel in these two long-term intellectual capitals together. As competition among the emerging economies is

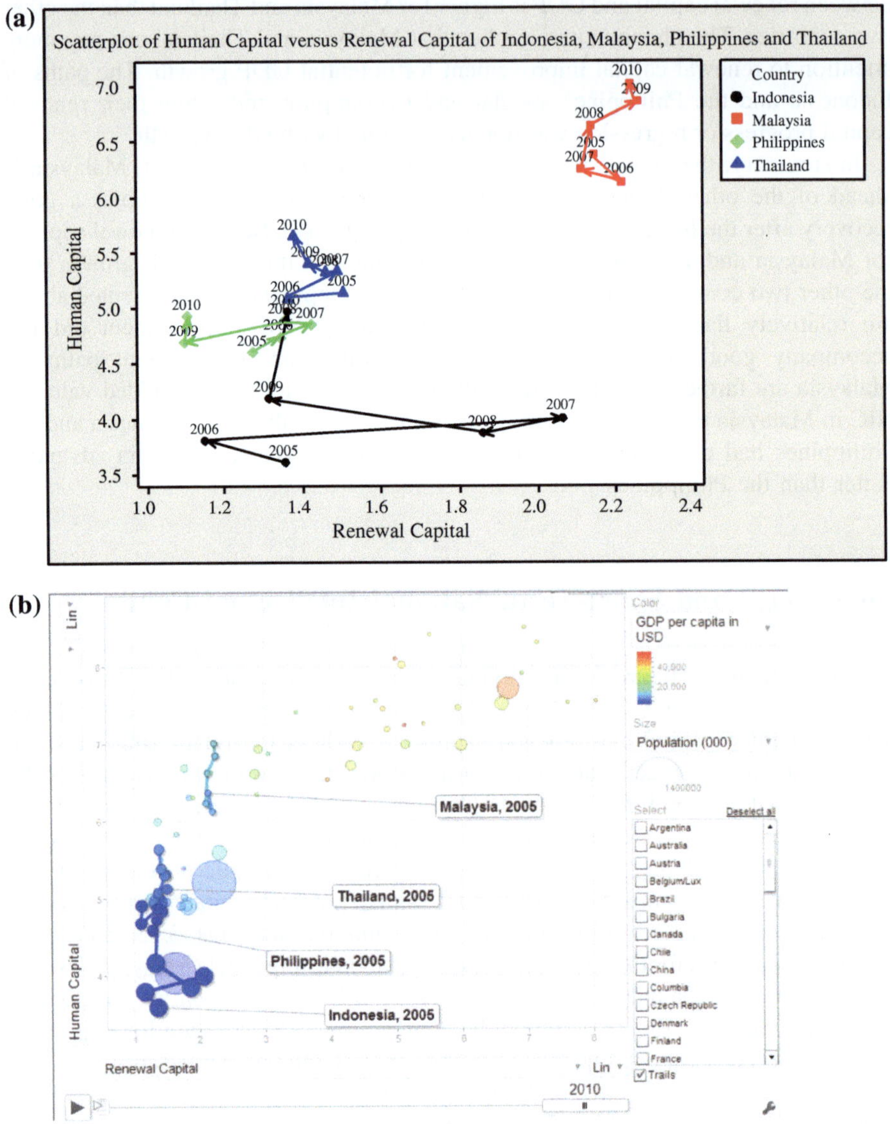

Fig. 3.13 **a** Human capital versus renewal capital for Indonesia, Malaysia, the Philippines, and Thailand. **b** Human capital versus renewal capital for Indonesia, Malaysia, the Philippines, and Thailand with background countries

likely to become more and more intense, these two graphs provide some perspectives for policy makers to ponder upon.

Figure 3.14a and b map market capital and process capital of the four economies on a coordinate plane. Market capital refers to the general assets embodied in a nation's relationship with international markets while process capital refers to

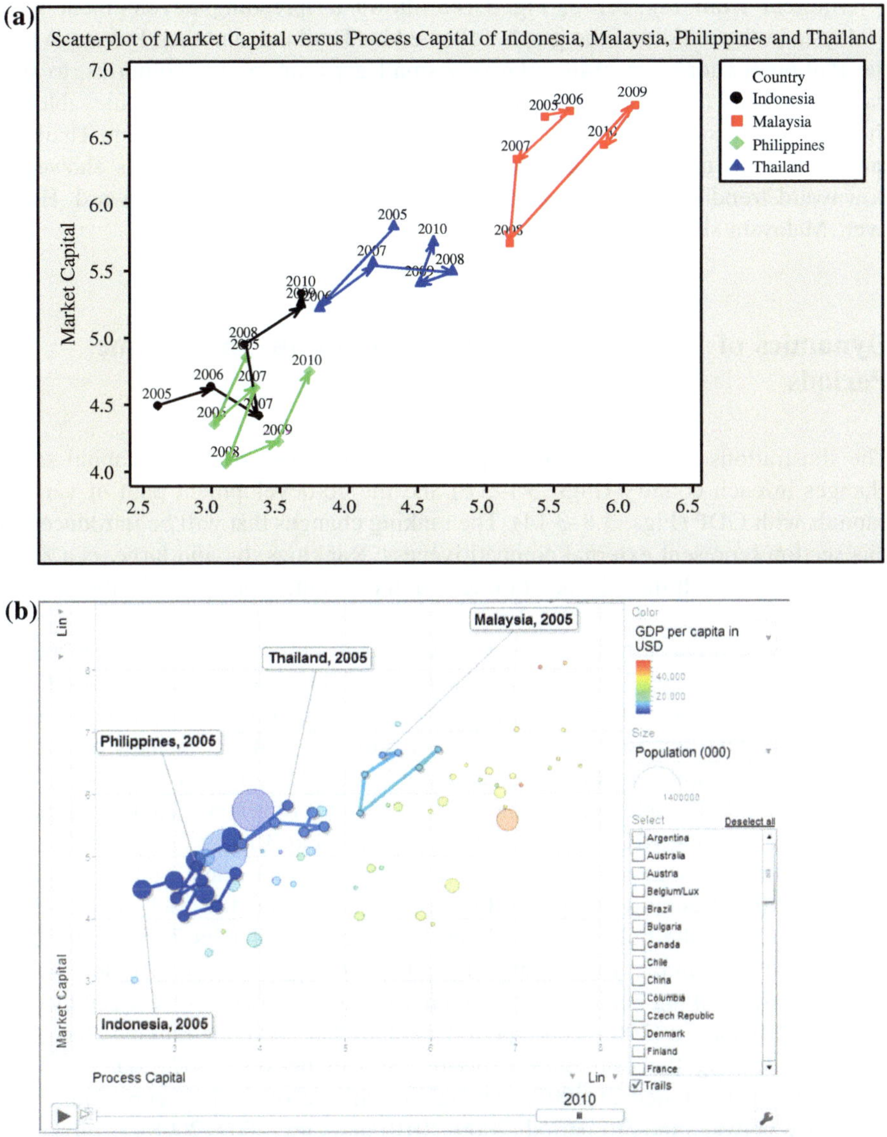

Fig. 3.14 **a** Market capital versus process capital for Indonesia, Malaysia, the Philippines, and Thailand. **b** Market capital versus process capital for Indonesia, Malaysia, the Philippines, and Thailand with background countries

national infrastructure, such as information systems and the number of days required to start a new business. For short-term competition, these are two types of capital that can be expected to produce faster results if a nation is willing to engage in more extensive investments.

Different from Fig. 3.13b, Fig. 3.14b shows a spreading development with Malaysia in the middle of the graph, followed by Thailand, and then Indonesia and the Philippines together. With relatively small gaps among the countries, to surpass Malaysia's market capital and process capital should be readily achievable for the other three countries. For this short-term oriented NIC, Indonesia and Thailand largely had an upward trend; whereas Malaysia and the Philippines showed a downward trend during the financial crisis and then rebounded afterward. However, Malaysia slid again in 2010.

Dynamics of National Intellectual Capital in Three Time Periods

The illustrations and graphs in the previous section describe NIC capital score changes in each country (Figs. 3.1–3.6) and the co-development path of various capitals with GDP (Figs. 3.8–3.14). The ranking changes that will be introduced in this section represent external competitiveness. Rankings, by and large, is a zero-sum game in which the advance of one country simultaneously marks the decline of another.

In order to probe the dynamics of NIC change before and after the financial crisis, we plotted Figs. 3.15–3.18 and Table 3.2 in three time periods: 2005–2006, 2007–2008, and 2009–2010. To have a clearer presentation, we separate the data in two sets. The first set contains capital scores and ranking changes of human capital, market capital, and process capital in Figs. 3.15, 3.16, 3.17, and 3.18. The second set exhibits capital scores and ranking changes of renewal capital, financial capital, and average NIC in Figs. 3.15, 3.16, 3.17, and 3.18.

The figures are mapped based on the mean capital scores and ranking changes of each period. Ranking changes in Figs. 3.15–3.18 are next to each capital score and copied from the bold-faced ranking difference of columns 2, 5, 7, and 9 of Table 3.2. For example, for the human capital ranking difference of Indonesia (1, 2, −1, 0), the ranking change of "1," representing the difference between the 3rd (2009–2010) and 1st (2005–2006) period, is plotted at 2005; the ranking change of "2," representing the difference between the 2nd period (2007–2008) and 1st (2005–2006), is plotted at 2007; the ranking change of "−1," representing the difference between the 3rd period (2009–2010) and 2nd (2007–2008), is plotted at 2009; and the ranking change of "0," representing the difference between the 3rd period (2009–2010) and 6-year average ranking (exhibited in Table 3.1), is plotted at 2010. Special attention can be paid to the negative numbers, which indicate that the level of a particular capital was higher before than after the financial crisis. Since it is easier to read figures than tables, we will describe the findings of each figure separately.

As shown in Fig. 3.15a and Table 3.2, Indonesia's human capital (1, 2, −1, 0) showed relatively small ranking changes. However, its market capital (13, 8, 5, 6)

(a)

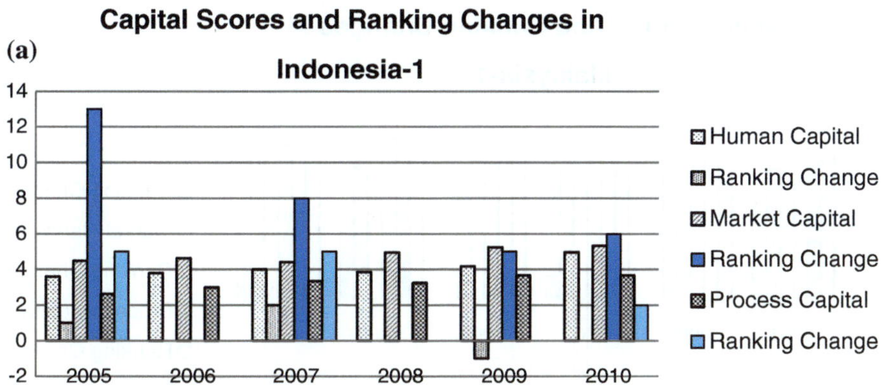

(b)

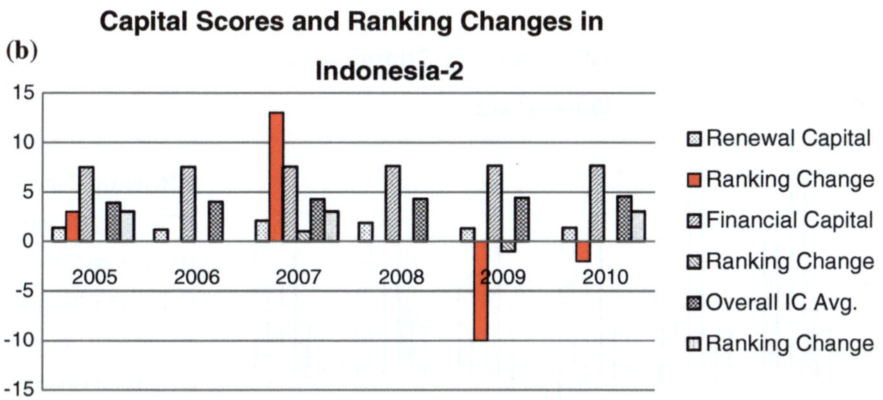

Fig. 3.15 **a** Human capital, market capital, process capital, and ranking changes in Indonesia. **b** Renewal capital, financial capital, average intellectual capital, and ranking changes in Indonesia

and process capital (5, 5, 0, 2) ranking gains show the largest scale of improvement among all types of ranking changes for the four countries over the course of the study. This finding reflects its resilience and recovery during and after the financial crisis as reported in Chap. 2.

Figure 3.15b shows that Indonesia had large-scale ranking changes in renewal capital (3, 13, −10, −2). The ten rank (−10) decline means Indonesia lost international competitiveness in renewal capital comparing the most recent 2009–2010 period with 2007–2008. In addition, its most recent renewal capital ranking (2009–2010) decreased by two ranks (−2) compared with its 6 year average ranking (Table 3.1). For its financial capital ranking, there was not much change (0, 1, −1, 0) in Indonesia. For the overall NIC, Indonesia had a relatively good progress (3, 3, 0, 3). In general, Indonesia increased its international competitiveness in terms of market capital, process capital, and NIC after the financial crisis. However, its already low renewal capital (rank 42 out of 48 in Table 3.1)

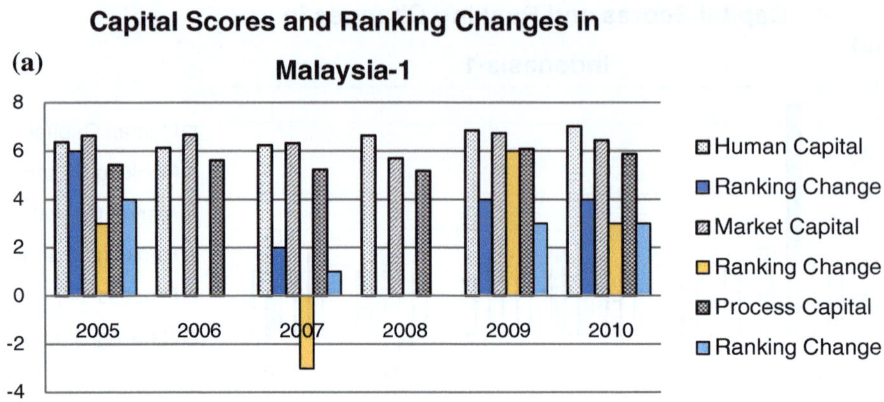

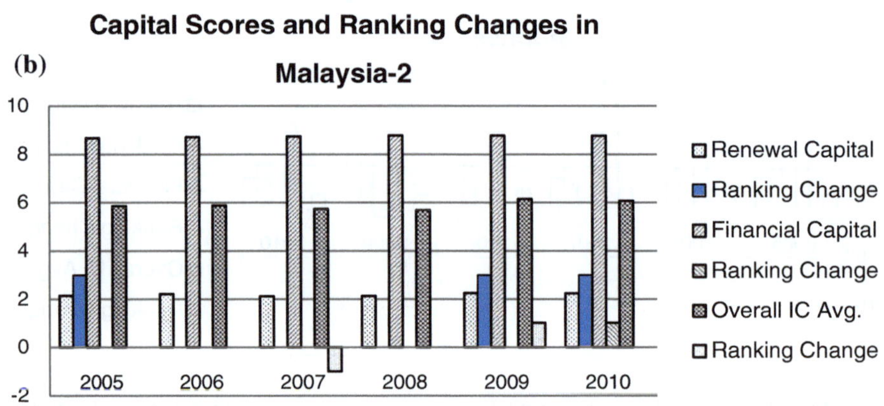

Fig. 3.16 **a** Human capital, market capital, process capital, and ranking changes in Malaysia. **b** Renewal capital, financial capital, average intellectual capital, and ranking changes in Malaysia

further lost international competitiveness even though there was not much of a score change (Fig. 3.4).

Figure 3.16a and Table 3.2 show that human capital (6, 2, 4, 4), market capital (3, −3, 6, 3), and process capital (4, 1, 3, 3) ranking progression in Malaysia are mostly positive, except one in market capital. The ranking decline (−3) indicates that Malaysia's market capital lost international competitiveness during the financial crisis, comparing the periods 2007–2008 and 2005–2006. However, it rebounded swiftly with 6 and 3 rank gains in the last two market capital ranking comparisons.

Figure 3.16b shows that Malaysia had relatively good renewal capital ranking gains (3, 0, 3, 3) among the four countries. However, its ranking changes in financial capital (0, 0, 0, 1) and NIC (0, −1, 1, 0) were minor. Overall, Malaysia

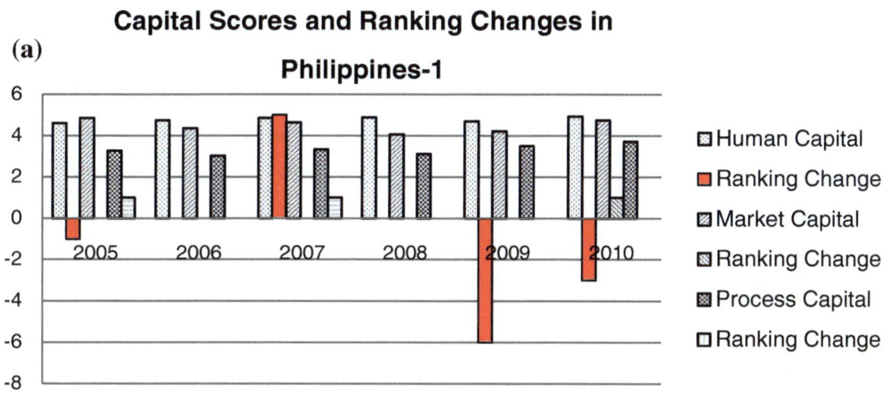

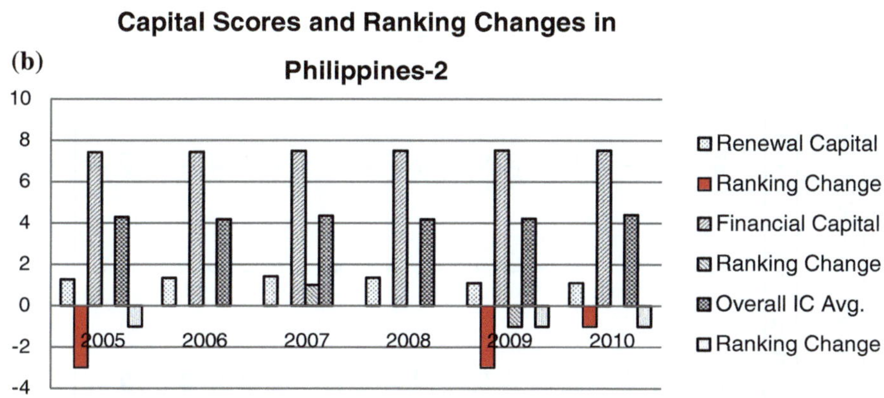

Fig. 3.17 **a** Human capital, market capital, process capital, and ranking changes in the Philippines. **b** Renewal capital, financial capital, average intellectual capital, and ranking changes in the Philippines

had the most positive ranking gains, representing international competitiveness, in various types of comparisons among the four countries.

Figure 3.17a and Table 3.2 show that the Philippines mainly lost human capital (−1, 5, −6, −3) international competitiveness after the financial crisis, with three out of four negative numbers. For market capital (0, 0, 0, 1) and process capital (1, 1, 0, 0), there was not much ranking change.

Figure 3.17b shows ranking decreases in renewal capital (−3, 0, −3, −1). For financial capital (0, 1, −1, 0) and NIC (−1, 0, −1, −1), the ranking changes were small. In general, the Philippines further lost international competitiveness in its already low human capital (rank 43 out of 48 in Table 3.1) and renewal capital (rank 47 out of 48 in Table 3.1) after the financial crisis.

Figure 3.18a and Table 3.2 show that Thailand generally had positive ranking changes in human capital (3, 2, 1, 3), market capital (4, 4, 0, 0), and process capital

Table 3.2 Ranking changes in three time periods for Indonesia, Malaysia, the Philippines, and Thailand

	1st period–3rd period	1st period 2005–2006	2nd period 2007–2008		3rd period 2009–2010		3rd period ranking versus overall NIC ranking	
	Difference #	Ranking	Ranking	Difference	Ranking	Difference	NIC 48 Ranking	Difference
Human capital								
Indonesia	**1**	48	46	**2**	47	**−1**	47	**0**
Malaysia	**6**	28	26	**2**	22	**4**	26	**4**
The Philippines	**−1**	45	40	**5**	46	**−6**	43	**−3**
Thailand	**3**	38	36	**2**	35	**1**	38	**3**
Market capital								
Indonesia	**13**	40	32	**8**	27	**5**	33	**6**
Malaysia	**3**	9	12	**−3**	6	**6**	9	**3**
The Philippines	**0**	39	39	**0**	39	**0**	40	**1**
Thailand	**4**	26	22	**4**	22	**0**	22	**0**
Process capital								
Indonesia	**5**	47	42	**5**	42	**0**	44	**2**
Malaysia	**4**	24	23	**1**	20	**3**	23	**3**
The Philippines	**1**	44	43	**1**	43	**0**	43	**0**
Thailand	**4**	36	31	**5**	32	**−1**	33	**1**
Renewal capital								
Indonesia	**3**	47	34	**13**	44	**−10**	42	**−2**
Malaysia	**3**	31	31	**0**	28	**3**	31	**3**
The Philippines	**−3**	45	45	**0**	48	**−3**	47	**−1**
Thailand	**0**	42	44	**−2**	42	**2**	43	**1**
Financial Capital								
Indonesia	**0**	46	45	**1**	46	**−1**	46	**0**
Malaysia	**0**	34	34	**0**	34	**0**	35	**1**

(continued)

Table 3.2 (continued)

	1st period–3rd period	1st period 2005–2006	2nd period 2007–2008		3rd period 2009–2010		3rd period ranking versus overall NIC ranking	
	Difference #	Ranking	Ranking	Difference	Ranking	Difference	NIC 48 Ranking	Difference
The Philippines	**0**	47	46	**1**	47	**−1**	47	**0**
Thailand	**0**	43	42	**1**	43	**−1**	43	**0**
NIC								
Indonesia	**3**	47	44	**3**	44	**0**	47	**3**
Malaysia	**0**	24	25	**−1**	24	**1**	24	**0**
The Philippines	**−1**	46	46	**0**	47	**−1**	46	**−1**
Thailand	**1**	34	34	**0**	33	**1**	34	**1**

Remarks
1. The second column compares the 3rd (2009–2010) period ranking with the 1st (2005–2006)
2. The fifth column compares the 2nd (2007–2008) period ranking with the 1st (2005–2006)
3. The seventh column compares the 3rd (2009–2010) period ranking with the 2nd (2007–2008)
4. The last column compares the most current 3rd period ranking (2009–2010) with the original 6-year average NIC48 ranking summarized in Table 3.1

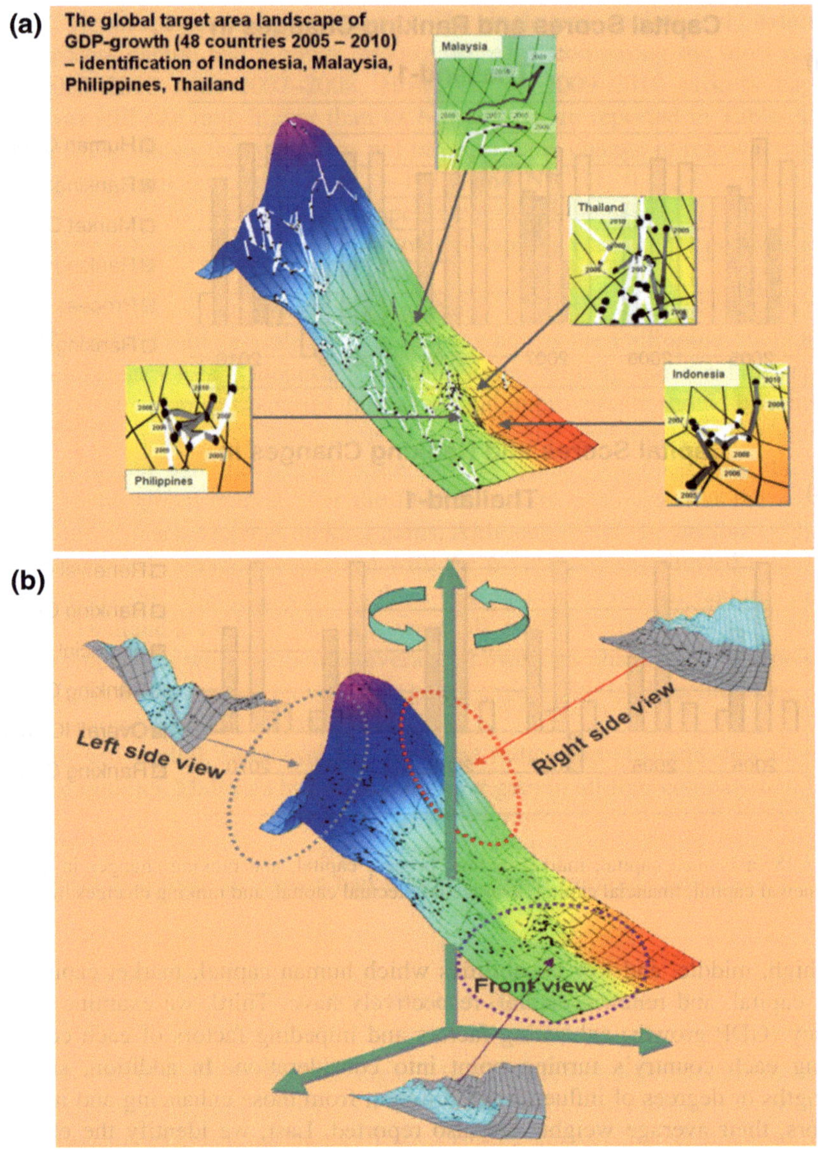

Fig. 3.19 **a** The NIC trail of Indonesia, Malaysia, the Philippines, and Thailand on a 3D 48-country landscape. **b** The potential rotation and partial presentation of the 3D formation

purple, dark blue, blue, green, yellow, and red is computer generated, according to GDP values, with purple representing high GDP and red low GDP. Figure 3.19b presents the potential rotation or partial presentation of the 3D formation in order to provide readers a better view for the focal area of discussion.

The relative NIC positions of Indonesia, Malaysia, the Philippines, and Thailand (pointed out with arrows) are located at different parts of the overall landscape. The NIC trail of Malaysia is located in the center, whereas those of the other three countries are at the lower central part of the 3D rectangular formation.

Figure 3.20a, b, and c form a set together. The areas of focus are shaded in light blue. Automated by the computer program to have a better view, the three figures are taken from front-to-left view as Fig. 3.19b indicates. Figure 3.20a presents four graphs indicating the high capability region of human capital, market capital, process capital, and renewal capital in explaining the GDP growth. High capability means the data points are 20 % above the mean value of each capital. This figure shows that none of the countries fall in the high capability region.

Figure 3.20b displays another four graphs indicating the middle capability region of each human capital, market capital, process capital, and renewal capital in explaining the GDP growth. Middle capability means the data points are within the top 50 % value of each capital. This figure shows that human capital, market capital, and process capital of Malaysia, and market capital of Thailand fall in the middle capability region.

Figure 3.20c presents the last four graphs in this set and indicates the low capability region of each human capital, market capital, process capital, and renewal capital in explaining the GDP growth. Low capability means the data points are 20 % below the mean value of each capital. This figure shows that capitals other than described in Fig. 3.20b fall in the low capability region.

In general, Fig. 3.20a, b, and c as a set explain that almost 75 % of the capitals (12 out of $4 \times 4 = 16$) of these four countries are in the low capability region in explaining GDP growth. These three figures demonstrate that these four countries are relatively less developed in national intangible assets among the 48 countries. In an era when intangible assets play an increasingly important role in national development, the messages revealed in these graphs deserve special attention for required actions.

Another set of figures, Fig. 3.21a, b, c, and d display efficiency enhancing or impeding factors that affect GDP growth before and after the NIC turning points for Indonesia, Malaysia, the Philippines, and Thailand, respectively. The white indicator boxes on the upper right display the results of the enhancing or impeding factors. We employed three or four rounds of data analysis, depending on whether the country has one or two NIC turning points. For instance, Malaysia's turning points are 2008 and 2009; therefore, we traced the explaining factors of 2005 against 2008 (starting point → the first turning point), 2007 against 2008 (one year before the turning point → the first turning point), 2008 against 2009 (one year before the turning point → the second turning point), and 2009 against 2010 (the second turning point → the ending point).

As an easy reference, we summarize in Table 3.3 two sets of results, each with the five key factors. If there is a clear percentage difference cutting point (such as less than 1 % in the white indicator boxes), the reported factors may be less than five. Results for the first set show the efficiency enhancing and impeding factors before the turning point; results for the second set show the efficiency enhancing and

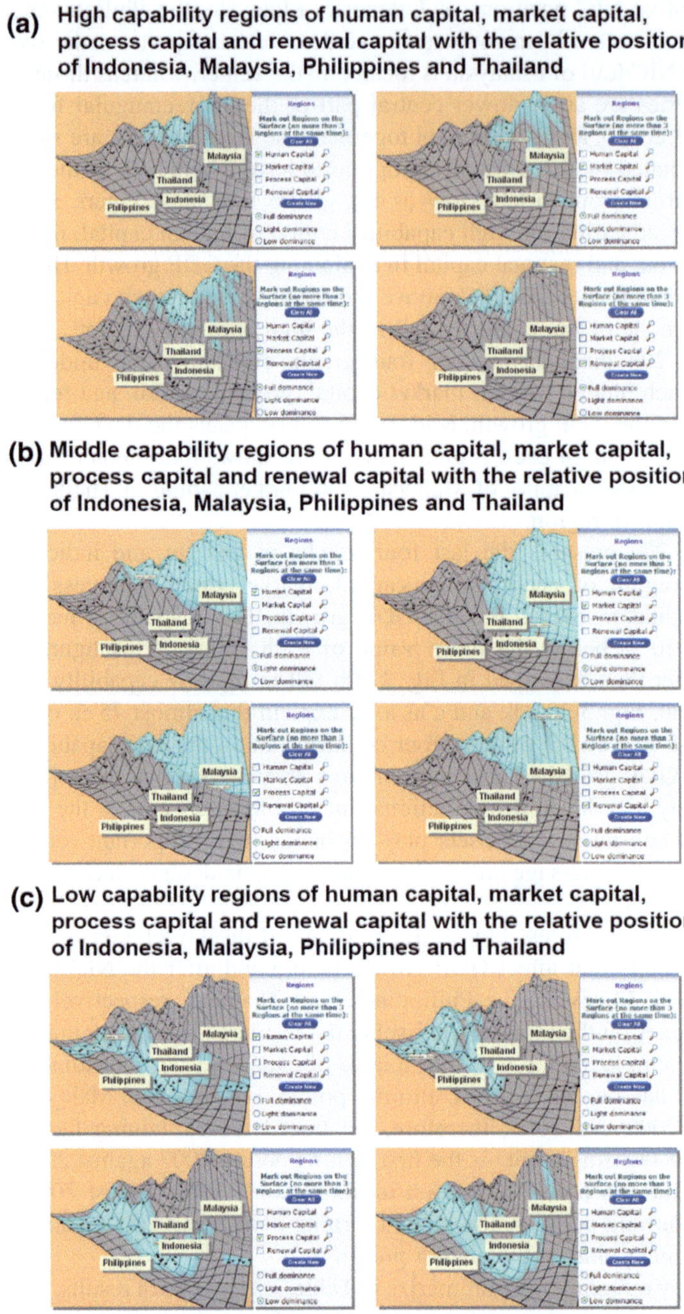

Fig. 3.20 **a** The high capability region of human capital, market capital, process capital, and renewal capital. **b** The middle capability region of human capital, market capital, process capital, and renewal capital. **c** The low capability region of human capital, market capital, process capital, and renewal capital

impeding indicators after the (2nd) turning point in italics. We also count the frequency of four more frequently displayed categories, namely government-related issues (G), human capital-related issues (H), market capital-related issues (M), and research and development issues (R&D). Since capital availability is a concern during the financial crisis, we particularly highlighted this factor as "G-C."

Figure 3.21a shows the 2007 turning point, the enhancing and impeding factors of Indonesia. The four rectangular 3D graphs on the left hand side of the figure indicate that all of Indonesia's human capital, market capital, process capital, and renewal capital fall into the low capability region (20 % below average).

Table 3.3 shows that in Indonesia, three impeding factors before the turning point were turned to enhancing factors after the turning point, whereas two factors had the opposite direction. The three positive direction factors include corporate tax encouragement, basic research, and globalization; the two negative direction factors are fair business competition environment and government efficiency. Export of goods remained an impeding factor before and after the turning point. The last row of Table 3.3 is the summary of the frequency count and indicates that more impeding factors fall in the category of government and market capital-related issues (4 counts each).

To reveal more thorough information regarding the effect of enhancing and impeding factors, we have calculated the average weight of the five enhancing and impeding factors and display the results at the two rows of "Factor #5". For instance, before the turning point the average weight of the five enhancing factors was 20.05 %, whereas the average weight of the five impeding factors was only 2.45 %. After the turning point, the average weight of impeding factors (5.42 %) is also smaller than that of the enhancing factors (23.61 %). In other words, the listed impeding factors did not pose too much threat to Indonesia from weighted influence point of view. However, the high frequency count category, such as government and market capital issues still deserve some attention.

Figure 3.21b shows the 2008 and 2009 turning points, the enhancing and impeding factors of Malaysia. The four rectangular 3D graphs on the left hand side of the figure indicate that Malaysia's human capital, market capital, and process capital fall into the middle capability region (top 50 %) and renewal capital is in the low capability region (20 % below average).

Table 3.3 shows that in Malaysia, government-related issues have 7 out of 10 frequency counts as impeding factors and none of them have been turned to enhancing factors after the turning point. According to the relatively high average weight (21.41 %) of impeding factors before the 2008 turning point, four government-related issues deserve special attention, including transparency of government policy, government efficiency, corporate tax encouragement, and convenience of establishing new firms. Cross-border ventures remained an impeding factor before and after the turning point.

Enhancing factors in Malaysia consist of four human capital-related issues and some fundamentals, such as public expenditure on education, pupil-teacher ratio, literacy rate, mobile phone subscribers, internet subscribers, and computers in use per capita. The average weight of enhancing factors (6.67 %) before the turning

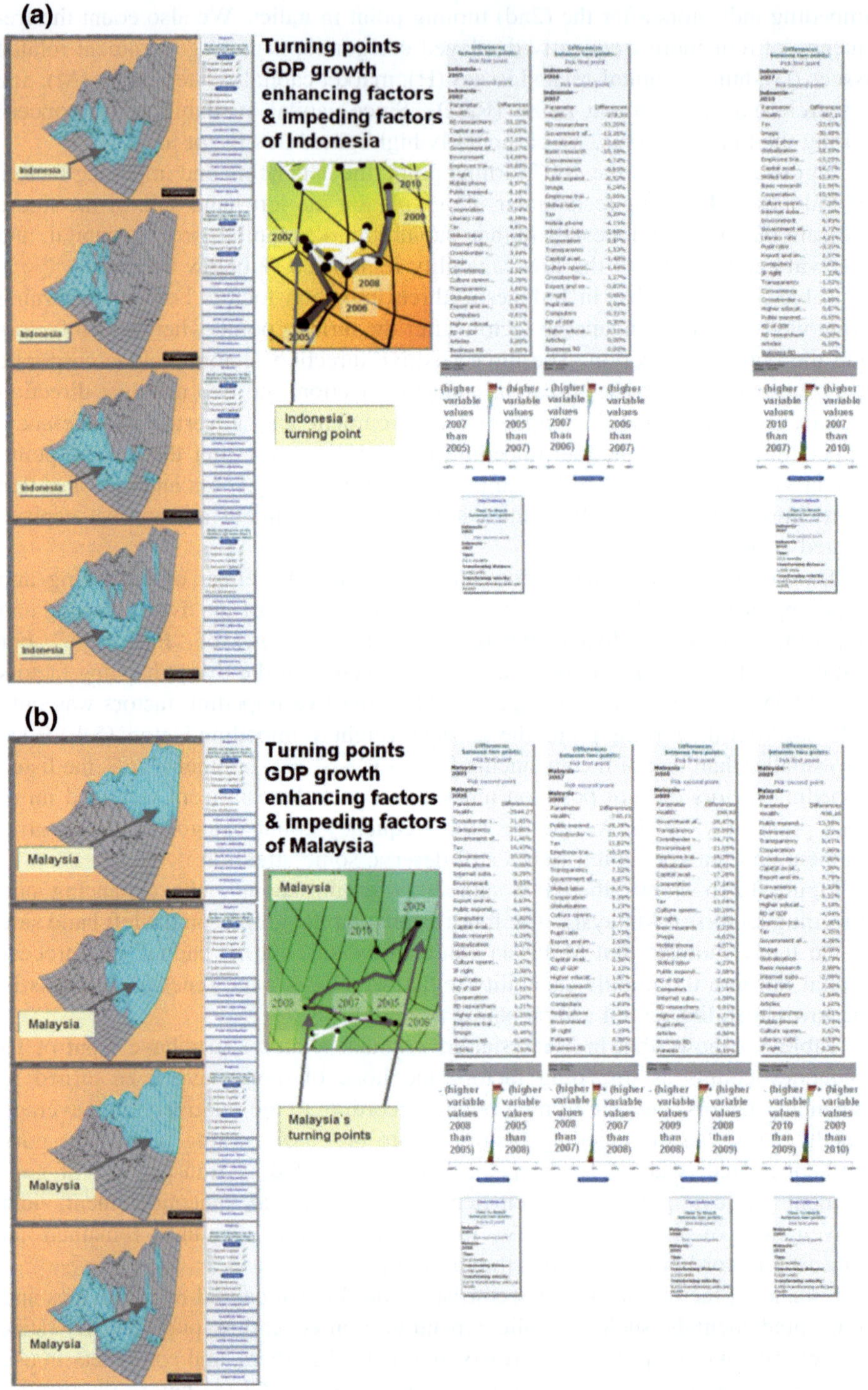

Fig. 3.21 **a** Turning point and GDP growth enhancing and impeding factors of Indonesia. **b** Turning points and GDP growth enhancing and impeding factors of Malaysia. **c** Turning points and GDP growth enhancing and impeding factors of the Philippines. **d** Turning point and GDP growth enhancing and impeding factors of Thailand

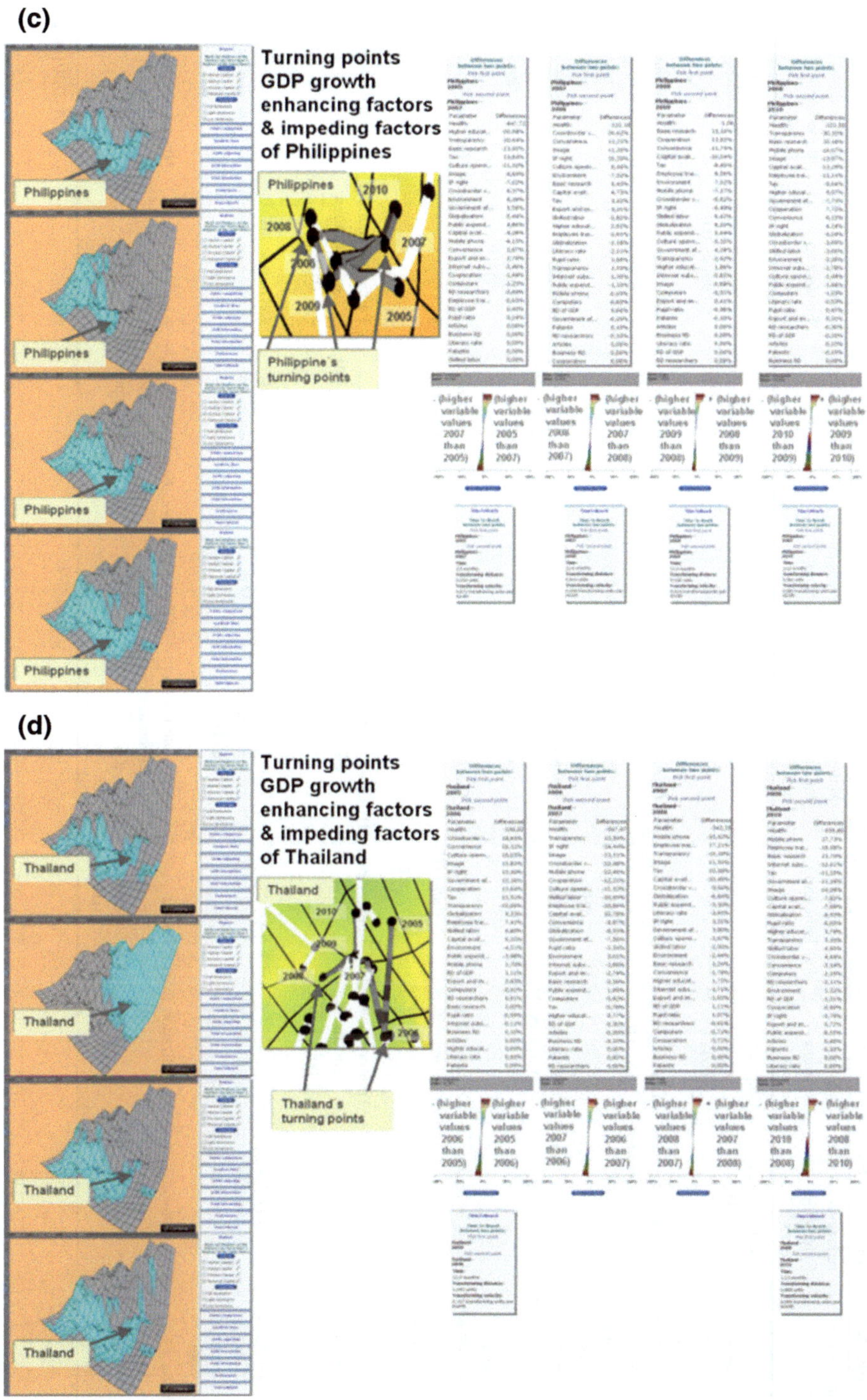

Fig. 3.21 continued

Table 3.3 Enhancing factors and impeding factors of GDP growth for Indonesia, Malaysia, the Philippines, and Thailand

Influencing factor	Indonesia Enhancing factors	Indonesia Impeding factors	Malaysia Enhancing factors	Malaysia Impeding factors	The Philippines Enhancing factors	The Philippines Impeding factors	Thailand Enhancing factors	Thailand Impeding factors
Factor #1 before (1st) turning point	R&D researchers (R&D)	Corporate tax encouragement (G)	Mobile phone subscribers	Cross-border ventures (M)	Higher education enrollment (H)	Transparency of government policy (G)	Transparency of government policy (G)	Cross-border ventures (M)
Factor #1 after (2nd) turning point	*Corporate tax encouragement* (G)	*Basic research* (R&D)	*Public expenditure on education* (H)	*Fair business competition environment* (G)	*Transparency of government policy* (G)	*Basic research* (R&D)	*Employee training* (H)	*Mobile phone subscribers*
Factor #2 before (1st) turning point	Capital availability (G-C)	Cross-border ventures (M)	Internet subscribers	Transparency of government policy (G)	Basic research (R&D)	Corporate tax encouragement (G)	Fair business competition environment (G)	Convenience of establishing new firms (G)
Factor #2 after (2nd) turning point	*Image of country* (M)	*Fair business competition environment* (G)	*Pupil–teacher ratio* (H)	*Transparency of government policy* (G)	*Mobile phone subscribers*	*Higher education enrollment* (H)	*Internet subscribers*	*Basic research* (R&D)
Factor #3 before (1st) turning point	Basic research (R&D)	Transparency of government policy (G)	Literacy rate (H)	Government efficiency (G)	Openness of culture (M)	Cross-border ventures (M)	Public expenditure on education (H)	Openness of culture (M)
Factor #3 after (2nd) turning point	*Mobile phone subscribers*	*Government efficiency* (G)	*R&D % GDP* (R&D)	*University-enter. cooperation* (R&D)	*Image of country* (M)	*University-enter. cooperation* (R&D)	*Corporate tax encouragement* (G)	*Higher education enrollment* (H)
Factor #4 before (1st) turning point	Government efficiency (G)	Globalization (M)	Public expenditure on education (H)	Corporate tax encouragement (G)	Image of country (M)	Fair business competition environment (G)	–	Image of country (M)

(continued)

Table 3.3 (continued)

Influencing factor	Indonesia Enhancing factors	Indonesia Impeding factors	Malaysia Enhancing factors	Malaysia Impeding factors	The Philippines Enhancing factors	The Philippines Impeding factors	Thailand Enhancing factors	Thailand Impeding factors
Factor #4 after (2nd) turning point	*Globalization* (M)	*Export of goods* (M)	*Image of country* (M)	*Cross-border ventures* (M)	*Capital availability* (G-C)	–	*Government efficiency* (G)	*Transparency of government policy* (G)
Factor #5 before (1st) turning point	Fair business competition environment (G)	Export of goods (M)	Computers in use per capita	Convenience of establishing new firms (G)	IP rights protection (R&D)	Government efficiency (G)	–	IP rights protection (R&D)
	(Average weight– 20.05 %) #	**(Average weight– 2.45 %) #**	**(Average weight– 6.67 %)**	**(Average weight– 21.41 %)**	**(Average weight– 12.46 %)**	**(Average weight– 10.53 %)**	**(Average weight– 6.18 %)**	**(Average weight– 16.47 %)**
Factor #5 after (2nd) turning point	*Employee training* (H) **(Average weight– 23.61 %)**	*IP rights protection* (R&D) **(Average weight– 5.42 %)**	*Internet subscribers* **(Average weight– 6.16 %)**	*Capital availability* (G-C) **(Average weight– 8.16 %)**	*Employee training* (H) **(Average weight– 17.35 %)**	– **(Average weight– 12.32 %)**	*Image of country* (M) **(Average weight– 12.70 %)**	*Cross-border ventures* (M) **(Average weight– 11.44 %)**
Category frequency count	G–4 H–1 M–2 R&D–2	G–4 H–0 M–4 R&D–2	G–0 H–4 M–1 R&D–1	G–7 H–0 M–2 R&D–1	G–2 H–2 M–3 R&D–2	G–4 H–1 M–1 R&D–2	G–4 H–2 M–1 R&D–0	G–2 H–1 M–4 R&D–2

Remarks: *(G)* government-related issues (total 27 counts), *(H)* human capital issues (11 counts), *(M)* market capital issues (18 counts), *(R&D)* research and development (12 counts)
Average weight of enhancing/impeding factor before and after the turning point

point is relatively small comparing with that of the impeding factors (21.41 %). A good sign in Malaysia is that the average weight of impeding factors after the 2009 turning point was reduced to 8.16 from 21.41 % before the 2008 turning point, reflecting improvement after the financial crisis.

Figure 3.21c shows the 2007, 2008, and 2009 turning points, the enhancing and impeding factors of the Philippines. The four rectangular 3D graphs on the left hand side of the figure indicate that all of the Philippine human capital, market capital, process capital, and renewal capital fall into the low capability region (20 % below average).

Table 3.3 shows that in the Philippines, government-related issues have 4 out of 10 frequency counts as impeding factors; however, transparency of government policy has been turned to enhancing factor after the second turning point. The average weight of impeding factors after the second turning point is higher than before the turning point (12.32 vs. 10.53 %). In addition, we include only three impeding factors after the second turning point due to the very small weight (less than 1 %) of the 4th and the 5th factors. The three impeding factors after the second turning point deserve great attention; they are basic research, higher education enrollment, and university-enterprise cooperation. Particularly, basic research and higher education enrollment have been turned from enhancing factors before the 2007 turning point to impeding factors after the 2008 turning point.

For enhancing factors, market capital-related issues, such as openness of culture and image of country, count more in the Philippines. Government, human capital, and R&D-related issues have two frequency counts each in the enhancing factors category, with a little higher average weight than the impeding factors.

Figure 3.21d shows the 2006 and 2008 turning points as well as the enhancing and impeding factors of Thailand. The four rectangular 3D graphs on the left hand side of the figure indicate that Thailand's market capital is at the middle capability region (top 50 %) and the rest human capital, process capital, and renewal capital fall into the low capability region (20 % below average).

Table 3.3 shows that in Thailand, market capital-related issues have 4 out of 10 frequency counts as impeding factors; however image of country has been turned to enhancing factor after the second turning point. The average weight of impeding factors before the 2006 turning point is higher than the weight after the 2008 turning point (16.47 vs. 11.44 %), indicating its need for improving the factors before the financial crisis including cross-border venture and convenience of establishing new firms.

For enhancing factors, government-related issues count more in Thailand. However, transparency of government policy has been turned from an enhancing factor before the turning point to an impeding factor after the turning point and deserves special attention.

To summarize Table 3.3 into an overall suggestion, we count the frequency of both enhancing and impeding factors by categories for all four countries. There are a total of 27 frequency counts of government-related issues (G), among which 10 are enhancing factors and 17 are impeding factors. Since government capital availability is generally tight during the financial crisis, we particularly mark the factor with (G-C). Out of the 27 government factors, 3 relate to capital availability. In Indonesia, capital availability is the second enhancing factor before the 2007 turning point, reflecting the fact that Indonesia was not short of capital before the financial crisis. Capital availability is the fifth impeding factor in Malaysia after the turning point, which is relatively minor when viewing from the much reduced average weight of 8.16 % from before the turning point of 21.41 %. In the Philippines, capital availability is the fourth enhancing factor after the turning point.

There are 11 counts of human capital issues (H), including 2 counts of impeding factors of higher education enrollment in both the Philippines and Thailand. There are 18 counts of market capital issues (M), including 11 counts of impeding factors concerning cross-border ventures, openness of culture, and export of goods. "Cross-border ventures" is an impeding factor for all four countries; particularly, it shows up as a problem both before and after the turning point for Malaysia and Thailand. For R&D there are 12 counts, among which impeding factors totaled 7 counts, including basic research, IP rights protection, and university–enterprise cooperation. Basic research is a concern in Indonesia, the Philippines, and Thailand; IP rights protection is a concern in Indonesia and Thailand, and university-enterprise cooperation is a concern in Malaysia and the Philippines. Generally speaking, government related- and market capital-related issues account more for impeding factors in these four countries.

Figure 3.22 identifies the efficiency drivers (positive term) for each individual country. Efficiency targeting is like benchmarking. Efficiency represents the GDP in this 3D software program. Since Japan has led the development of Asia for decades and has been the example for rising economies like Korea and Taiwan, it serves as a good benchmark for these four Southeast Asian countries. As such, Japan's GDP is the efficiency target in Fig. 3.22. In this figure, the stacked small horizontal stripes are the deficiency factors of each economy benchmarked against Japan's GDP in 2010. The length of the stripes represents the degree of deficiency. For easier comparison, we list the first five deficiency factors of each country in Table 3.4.

With Japan being used as the benchmarking country, irrespective to the sequence of deficiency, the common areas (in frequency count) that these four countries need to improve include patents (4 counts), R&D % GDP (4 counts), business R&D (3 counts), internet subscribers (3 counts), computers in use per capita (3 counts), and higher education enrollment (2 counts). From Table 3.4, Malaysia as the most advanced country in this country cluster has R&D-related issues as its first four efficiency drivers and the fifth one is higher education enrollment. This result reveals the need for Malaysia to develop its long-term NIC—human capital and renewal capital—when benchmarking Japan. Different from Malaysia, the rest three less developed countries have more fundamental factors—internet subscribers and computers in use per capita—as their efficiency drivers, indicating they still need to invest more in building a more facilitating environment for future national development.

Based on the average deficiency (negative term) percentage reported in Table 3.4, Indonesia has the longest distance (−79.67 %) to achieve the target

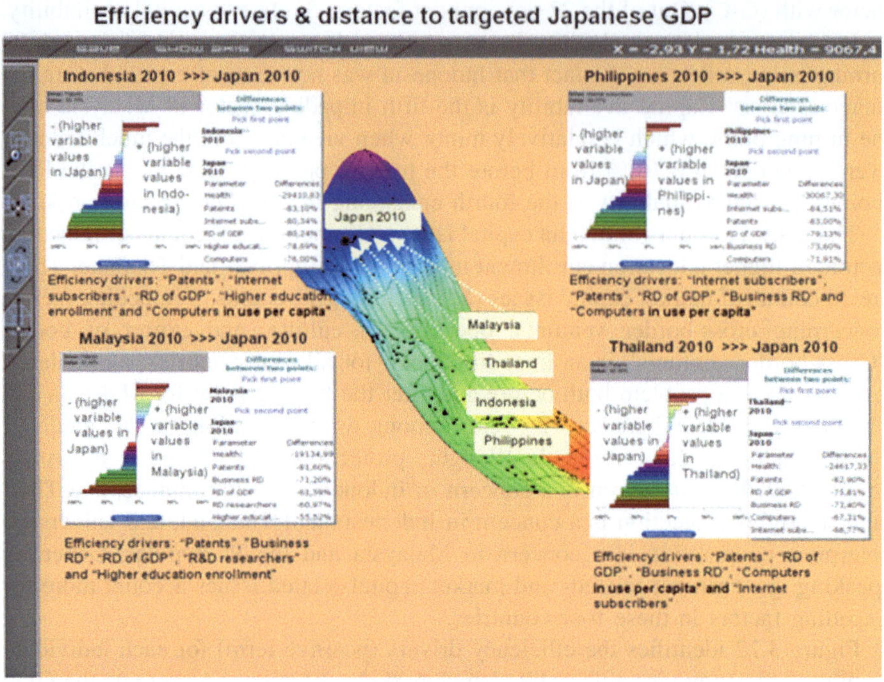

Fig. 3.22 Efficiency drivers and distance to targeted GDP of Japan

Table 3.4 The first five efficiency drivers targeting GDP of Japan

Efficiency driver	Indonesia	Malaysia	Philippines	Thailand
Factor #1	Patents	Patents	Internet subscribers	Patents
Factor #2	Internet subscribers	Business R&D	Patents	R&D % GDP
Factor #3	R&D % GDP	R&D % GDP	R&D % GDP	Business R&D
Factor #4	Higher education enrollment	R&D researchers	Business R&D	Computer in use per capita
Factor #5	Computers in use per capita	Higher education enrollment	Computers in use per capita	Internet subscribers
Average deficiency percentage of the above 5 drivers	−79.67 %	−66.18 %	−78.43 %	−73.24 %

GDP (Japan's), followed by the Philippines (−78.43 %), Thailand (−73.24 %), and Malaysia (−66.18 %).

The added value of the above 3D trajectory analysis is to (1) display the NIC trails of the discussed countries on a 48-country landscape; (2) locate the capability region of the four individual capitals for each country; (3) highlight NIC turning points, details of the enhancing or impeding factors, and the dynamics of factor changes for each country; and (4) calculate the distance that each country has to progress in order to achieve the benchmark GDP and identify the first five key factors to reach this goal. This section supplements the previous sections by looking into the contribution of each individual indicator in each year, rather than from the perspective of average scores and average rankings.

In this chapter, we reported our research findings in layman terms with graphs and tables of various types for easier understanding. This study on national intangible assets has uncovered some important findings that are not apparent in other GDP-related studies. For instance, we have graphically shown the NIC development paths of how Indonesia gradually caught up with the Philippines, which may partially explain the jump of Indonesia's global competitiveness from the world rank of number 74 in 2005–2006 to 46 in 2011–2012.

Chapter 4
Beyond the 2008 Global Financial Crisis

This chapter reports activities after 2010, a time line regarded as the aftermath of the 2008 global financial crisis which was formally announced to be over at the end of 2009 (Kehoe 2010; OECD 2010). Although some European countries were still boggled in sovereign debt trouble after 2010 (Greece requested another bailout in early 2012 and Spain asked for external financial assistance in June 2012), we use 2010 as a cutoff point in order to be consistent with the reports of other country clusters in this booklet series.

From the statistics introduced in Chaps. 2 and 3, economic situations of these four countries began to recover in the last quarter of 2009 under the support of each individual country's stimulus efforts, the gradual revival of global demands, and their relatively resilient financial systems after the 1997 Asian crisis. The western financial turmoil of 2008 has not left the economies of Indonesia, Malaysia, the Philippines and Thailand unscathed, yet these four countries have shown good recoveries.

According to OECD (2011), the overall growth impetus remains robust in the ASEAN countries, underpinned by strong domestic demand, large-scale investments in infrastructure, and buoyant private consumption. During the first quarter of 2011, the total capital inflows into the six ASEAN countries (Indonesia, Malaysia, the Philippines, Singapore, Thailand and Vietnam) amounted to more than US$40 billion. The growth momentum for the Emerging Asia (the six ASEAN countries plus China and India) as a whole is also robust with an average growth rate of 8.2 % in 2011 (OECD 2011). However from the second quarter of 2011, the notably reduced confidence in the US fiscal policy and continued Euro-area debt crisis cast a shadow over Asian economies, yet with limited impact.

Nevertheless, two large-scale natural disasters, the earthquake and ensuing tsunami in Japan as well as the floods in Thailand affected the region adversely. The earthquake had a temporary impact on activity and exports in some Asian countries including Indonesia, the Philippines, and Thailand. The unprecedented scale of floods in Thailand has added to downside risks in the region. Even though the IMF was gloomy about the world economy and cut its forecast for global

C. Y.-Y. Lin et al., *National Intellectual Capital and the Financial Crisis in Indonesia, Malaysia, The Philippines, and Thailand*, SpringerBriefs in Economics,
DOI: 10.1007/978-1-4614-7943-7_4,

economic growth for 2012 to 3.3 from 4 % (Kuroda 2012), growth of these four countries continues.

In what follows, in the sequence of Indonesia, Malaysia, the Philippines and Thailand, we briefly describe what had happened in each individual country after 2010 with some prior reasons.

Indonesia

Indonesia's economy withstood this global crisis very well and outperformed most of its regional neighbors. The main reasons include a moderate but timely fiscal impulse, successful macroeconomic management, low reliance on international trade with advanced countries, low exposure to toxic assets, and strong economic fundamentals (CIA 2012; OECD 2010). As a result of the consolidation and restructuring process initiated after the 1997 Asian economic collapse, the Indonesian financial sector was generally solid and performed well at the outset of the 2008 financial crisis (Ziegenhain 2010). These characteristics made the Indonesian economy less vulnerable to advanced economies' financial and economic turmoil. The country has also benefited from its increasing integration with other ASEAN economies, and more recently with China. By the end of 2009, the Indonesian stock market had restored all of the substantial losses associated with the crisis with its inflation declined to 2.78 % (McCulloch and Grover 2010).

After the crisis, increasing investments by both local and foreign investors also supported its solid growth. With prudent management and robust economic growth, Indonesian fiscal achievements have been significant. Its debt-to-GDP ratio in recent years has declined steadily from its peak of 90 % in 2000 to less than 30 % in 2009 (OECD 2010). In addition, owing to its increasingly robust GDP growth and sound fiscal stewardship, two of the three leading credit agencies have upgraded credit ratings for Indonesia's sovereign debt to one notch below investment grade (CIA 2012; OECD 2010). Based on IMF, by November 2011 Indonesia's international reserve has achieved US$114.502 billion, up from US$51.6 billion at the end of 2008.

After the 2008 financial crisis, Indonesia's reform measures have put greater emphasis on improving the entrepreneurial environment, enhancing regional competitiveness, and creating a more vibrant private sector through decentralization (Heritage 2012). However, in late 2010, increasing inflation driven by higher and volatile food prices, posed an increasing challenge to economic policymakers and threatened to push millions of the near-poor below the poverty line (CIA 2012).

For continuous reforms, finding the fiscal room to finance the expansion of growth-enhancing programs, such as investments in infrastructure, education at the secondary level, increasing coverage of formal social protection, and health insurance require enhancing tax enforcements and eliminating energy subsidies (OECD 2010). To achieve the objective of 7.0–7.7 % growth by 2014 set by the Indonesian government in its Medium Term Development Plan, further institutional changes, including a rapid implementation of bureaucratic reforms, decentralization, capacity building at the local level, and improvement in efficiency and economic governance are pre-requisites to meet these ambitious economic development goals (OECD 2010).

Malaysia

In retrospect, the Malaysian central bank helped limit Malaysia's exposure to riskier financial instruments and the global financial crisis by maintaining healthy foreign exchange reserves through a well-developed regulatory regime (CIA 2012). The consolidation and restructuring of the banking industry, improved governance structure, risk management framework, infrastructure and practices, and the capacity building after the Asian financial crisis have significantly strengthened Malaysia's financial fundamentals. The central bank of Malaysia has been proactive to ensure the financial stability during this round of financial crisis. Measures to provide undisrupted flow of funds to the real sector include its engagements with various financial institutions, trade associations and businesses, beginning as far back as early 2008 when conditions in the global economy appeared to be worsening (Ibrahim 2010). In addition, the central bank also ensured adequate US dollar liquidity to facilitate trade-related transactions and investment activities by arranging bilateral and multilateral currency swaps with regional countries and with the People's Bank of China.

Several regulations also facilitated the recovery of Malaysia's economy from the financial crisis. For example, by law all foreign institutions in Malaysia need to be locally incorporated, with capital committed to support Malaysian operations and obligations (Ibrahim 2010). Such requirement has limited the contagion effects of foreign banks in trouble. In addition, the funding sources for businesses are evenly balanced between the equity and bond markets and the banking sector, thus directing credit risk concentration away from the banking system, which in turn provides the banking system with added capacity to withstand stress and shocks. Furthermore, credit risks were retained within institutions' balance sheets, which served to align incentives with prudent risk-taking and ensured that lending institutions continued to vigilantly assess the repayment capacity of borrowers and monitor the quality of the loan throughout its tenure. As a result, overall confidence and stability in the Malaysian financial sector has been preserved throughout the period of this global financial crisis (Ibrahim 2010).

Particularly, the Malaysian government has established a Project Management Unit to ensure and accelerate the disbursement of the development expenditure, with a full understanding that the key successful factor of the stimulus plan lies on timely implementation (Abidin and Rasiah 2009). Such governance schemes indeed efficiently help stabilize the economic contraction. Although exports of electronics, oil and gas, palm oil and rubber still remain a significant driver of the economy, Malaysian government is continuing its efforts to boost domestic demand and reduce the economy's dependence on exports (CIA 2012). Continued expansion in domestic demand and increased external demand led to Malaysia's strong growth of 10.1 % in the first quarter of 2010 (Ibrahim 2010). In November 2011, its international reserve has reached US$130.978 billion (Global finance 2012), up from US$91.6 billion at the end of 2008.

For future development, Malaysia has launched an aggressive program after the financial crisis. So far, Malaysia has made considerable progress but remains a middle-income country and is still struggling to achieve its aspiration of becoming a high-income nation by 2020. To jump-start the effort, Malaysia announced a government transformation program in January 2010, aimed at delivering big results fast in the public services. In October 2010, the Economic Transformation Program (ETP), a road map to lead Malaysia to achieve its 2020 goals, was promoted nationwide. The program targets annual growth of 6 % and a doubling of gross national income (GNI) per capita to US$15,000, in order to meet the World Bank standard for a high-income country (Daly and Singham 2011).

The Philippines

In general, the Philippines had relatively low economic development compared with the other three countries; thus it was less impacted by this round of global financial crisis (CIA 2012). The Philippines' GDP grew 7.3 % in 2010, spurred by consumer demand, a rebound in exports and investments, and election-related spending. The government has had little difficulty issuing debt both locally and internationally to finance its deficits. In September 2010, the U.S. Secretary of State signed a US$434 million Millennium Challenge Corporation (MCC) grant for the Philippines to fund infrastructure and rural development programs to reduce poverty and spur economic growth (Cheng et al. 2010).

Based on the ING Investor Dashboard Survey (2010), investors showed confidence in the Philippine economy over the first two quarters of 2010. In 2010, record high amounts of remittances from overseas Filipino workers, plus the strengthening of its currency the Peso against the US dollar have brought about consumption-driven growth. Infrastructure investments were also a key priority of the government after the financial crisis. In 2010, the Philippine Stock Exchange index picked up significantly in the third quarter with a 22 % growth rate from 12 % in the second quarter. In the third quarter of 2010, local and foreign investors alike have reflected this optimism by pumping more money into Philippine stocks. Development plans have been laid out emphasizing education, health, conditional cash transfers for the poor, and other social spending programs. In addition, the government relies on the private sector to finance important infrastructure projects for more efficient and long-term development.

The new government has vowed to focus on improving tax collection efficiency—rather than imposing new taxes—as a part of its good governance platform. After the financial crisis, the Philippine budget emphasizes long-term development, including education, health, and other social spending programs. The government also promotes the private sector to finance important infrastructure projects to enhance efficiency. It also relies on the Asia Investment Infrastructure Fund (AIIF) to prioritize the funding of infrastructure projects (Yap et al. 2009). With such external financial support, the Philippines will be in a better position to push for national growth.

Since the beginning of 2011, a myriad of external shocks have affected the Philippine economy, starting from the Middle East and North Africa crisis and the resulting high oil prices, to the Japan earthquake and Thailand floods tragedies with their resulting supply chain disruptions, and the overall weakness of the world economy due in large part to the weaknesses in the European and U.S. economies. Despite the general world economic troubles, the Philippines is continuing to grow with a remarkably good economic outlook. In November 2011, international reserves of the Philippines reached US$75.17 billion (Global finance 2012), up from US$37.55 billion at the end of 2008. Its economy grew by 3.7 % in the fourth quarter of 2011, and from 3.1 and 3.6 % in the second and third quarters. However, the corresponding full year 2011 real GDP growth of 3.7 % is still lower than the 7.6 % rate of 2010 (PBBC 2012).The acceleration in public construction expenditure grew by 49.4 % in the fourth quarter to make up for government under spending. Accelerated public expenditures and disbursements continued well into 2012 and beyond.

In the Philippines, investment is expected to post strong growth in 2012, despite the global economic uncertainties. Especially, the construction sector will get a boost from public construction and from the Private–Public Partnership program in 2012. Expanded investments in energy; mining; low-cost housing and office buildings; and the industries in the priority areas—agribusiness, consumer durables, information technology (IT), health and wellness, transport, telecommunications, and especially tourism—all contribute positively to the country's economic growth in 2012 (PBBC 2012). The Philippines also benefited through the continued robust performance of the business process outsourcing industries. In the second half of 2012, the manufacturing sector is expected to post a remarkable growth as the food sector further expands and the electronic industry registers higher growth. The new government projected 5–6 % real GDP growth in 2012 (PBBC 2012).

Nevertheless, many analysts expect that the global economic recovery might stall in 2012 due to the growing concerns over Europe. The Philippine government is also closely following the economic developments in the U.S. and China, recognizing the spillover risk that China could slow down as well.

Thailand

In 2010, Thailand's economy expanded 7.6 %, its fastest pace since 1995, as exports rebounded from their depressed 2009 level (CIA 2012). Several reasons led to Thailand's fast recovery from the 2008 financial crisis, including good bank structure, sound housing finance industry, the effect of stimulus packages, and fast recovery in the Asian region.

The Thai housing and housing finance industry learned its lesson during the 1997 Asian financial crisis and subsequently successfully implemented safeguards against bubble-like booms or external shocks. The banking industry became much more cautious in their lending when providing project financing to housing developers and mortgage loans to individual borrowers. They implemented prudent mortgage lending practices including income, employment and National Credit Bureau verifications. No banks were providing US-type sub-prime loans (Kritayanavaj 2008).

Overall, nearly US$4.7 billion of stimulus spending in two packages had a profound effect in helping expand the Thai economy in 2010 (Chirathivat and Mallikamas 2010). In addition, the resuming demand of the fast recovered Asian economies, such as China, Korea, Singapore, and Taiwan prompted the increase of exports in Thailand as well.

In 2011, Thailand's economic momentum remained sound and the government had mapped its structural policy focus, including improving the outcome of education and reducing urban–rural disparities, enhancing agricultural productivity and improving jobs in the far sector, and speeding up the reform of state-owned enterprises through improving governance and management (OECD 2011). Although Thailand's supply chain was disrupted due to Japan's March 2011 earthquake, the effect is proven to be limited and temporary (Trairatvorakul 2011). The vehicle production for Thailand recovered in late May 2011. Domestic demand, both consumption and investment continues to be strong as underpinned by a high level of farm income, high employment, and good consumer and business confidence with a favorable credit condition. Tighter resource utilization and the accelerated capacity utilization rate in the vehicle sector from the second half of 2011 have reflected the country's vibrant economic activities. In November 2011, Thailand's international reserve reached US$180.113 billion (IMF 2012; Global Finance 2012), up from US$106 billion in December 2008 (Verghis and Bhaopichitr 2008).

With the economy of Thailand booming, the government shifted its concern about inflation to increasing the country's productivity. Particularly, the Bank of Thailand highlighted the importance of prioritizing government policies and spending (Trairatvorakul 2011). Priority should be given to productivity enhancement projects and spending should be selective and targeted to certain areas to ensure policy effectiveness.

In the second quarter of 2012, Thailand's GDP increased 4.2 % from a year earlier. However, the government also signaled growth in the second half of 2012 to be weaker than previously forecasted as a global slowdown hurts exports. The gross domestic product was forecasted to expand 5.5–6 %, compared with a previous growth range of 5.5–6.5 % and forecast for export growth reduced to 7.3 from 15.1 % on concern Europe's crisis will dampen demand (Yuvejwattana and Heath 2012). To boost growth, the Thai government has raised minimum wages and pledged to spend more than US$63.5 billion (Bt 2 trillion) on infrastructure and water-management projects over the next seven years to prevent a repeat of the flood disaster, which killed more than 700 people and cost the economy US$44.5 billion (Bt 1.4 trillion) (Yuvejwattana and Heath 2012).

Chapter 5
Future Perspective and Policy Implications

By the middle of 2012, more than three years have passed since the outbreak of the 2008 global financial crisis. Although some countries in the European Union are still in deep financial trouble, it is time to reflect upon what happened during the past few years and what can be learned from this crisis for future implications. The economic crisis provides an ideal opportunity to examine the soundness of a nation's economic system and the effectiveness of national governance for building a more robust economy in the future.

Global recovery started in 2010. However, recovery continued to be stagnant, mainly due to sovereign debt problems in Europe and a modest recovery in the U.S. In January 2012, the International Monetary Fund (IMF) announced that global recovery was threatened by intensifying strains in the Euro area; thus financial conditions have deteriorated, growth prospects have dimmed, and downside risks have escalated (IMF 2012). The Euro area economy was expected to go into a mild recession in 2012. The effects of bank deleveraging on the real economy may surface again and the impact of additional fiscal consolidation may heighten.

Even growth in developing economies that had traditionally remained resilient was expected to slow down because of the worsening external environment and a weakening of internal demand (IMF 2012).

In this chapter, we first present the prospects of these four Southeast Asian countries, and then describe the potential challenges they may face in the future. The prospects and challenges are meant to provide points of thought for discussion and do not represent an exhaustive list. This chapter finishes with some policy implications.

Prospects

A side effect of the 2008 financial crisis for the Southeast Asia region is that the crisis facilitated an increasing integration of the ASEAN member countries. During the crisis, member countries had a deeper understanding that they should

C. Y.-Y. Lin et al., *National Intellectual Capital and the Financial Crisis in Indonesia, Malaysia, The Philippines, and Thailand*, SpringerBriefs in Economics,
DOI: 10.1007/978-1-4614-7943-7_5,

support each other more, rather than depending heavily upon advanced western countries. The ASEAN+3 (adding China, Japan and Korea) financial cooperation in the future will further promote the development of domestic financial markets to facilitate the intermediation of Asian savings within the region, and to attract foreign investment. Such alternative sources of funding would reduce Asia's reliance on foreign currency borrowing and thus reduce the risk exposure of the region to currency mismatches. As each individual country has its own systems and resources, we briefly describe the prospects of each country as follows.

Indonesia

Indonesia's future prospect still relies on its sound and stable macroeconomic and political environment. Its favorable growth prospects and healthy public finances have offered Indonesia a unique opportunity to pursue its reform agenda and achieve lasting, strong, and inclusive growth (OECD 2010). As a member of the G20, Indonesia plays an increasingly important role in international economic policy discussions, which will certainly facilitate its growth in the future.

Knowing that a sound financial system helps a nation successfully carry out its development plans, the Bank of Indonesia is seeking to improve the efficiency of its monetary policy transmission mechanism. To achieve national planned goals, the government is removing obstacles to bank lending, developing long-term debt instruments, and facilitating public–private collaboration (OECD 2010). In Indonesia's Medium Term Development Plan, the government also announced significant investment plans—amounting to 5 % of GDP on average over five years, of which 64 % is to be financed through private funds, in the form of public–private partnerships. The government is also committed to alleviating poverty and has set an ambitious target of lowering the poverty rate from 13.3 % in March 2010 to 8–10 % by 2014 (OECD 2010).

Aggressively, Indonesia is also shifting attention in the design of its social-protection programs from crisis mitigation to strengthening support for vulnerable households to help them pull themselves out of poverty, link social protection to sustained improvements in social outcomes, and equip the poor with the means to prevent a long-lasting fall into poverty following adverse income shocks (OECD 2010).

In addition, the higher value-added creative industry also has an increasing role in Indonesia. According to the Creative Economy 2010 report, the creative industry in Indonesia contributed 4.7 % of the national GDP in 2006 and absorbed 3.7 million workers, equal to 4.7 % of the total workforce in 2008. Efforts in promoting the creative industry also cast a promising future for Indonesia.

Malaysia

During the financial crisis, Malaysia planned for short-term stimulus measures as well as long-term development under the guidance of their Millennium Development Goals (MDGs). The following thrusts should help Malaysia establish a sounder economy for resisting future external shock and for bringing prosperity to its society.

The Malaysian government has embarked on restructuring the economy and improving its competitiveness. Capacity building for the future covers investments, off budget projects, creative arts, and the effective management of government financial resources. Malaysia also continues to pursue liberalization, enhancing the entrepreneurial and investment environments. Specific measures on investment include increasing the funds for domestic investments, dedicating more funds to projects in infrastructure, telecommunication, technology, biotechnology, tourism, agriculture, and life sciences. Recently, policy announcements have been made to deregulate the Foreign Investment Committee guidelines (Abidin and Rasiah 2009). For instance, domestic equity requirements used to restrict foreign investment have been eliminated to improve investment freedom. As a result, Malaysia's economy freedom score is above the world average (Heritage 2012).

To mitigate the effects of the crisis on the poor and low income groups, the government reallocated the budget to support social sectors and set up targeted programs to serve three objectives: alleviate poverty, make adjustment programs more politically acceptable, and undertake institutional reforms. In addition, several measures are focused specifically on human development, such as providing training and creating employment opportunities, extending financial support for education at Masters and PhD levels, and attracting skilled workers by granting permanent residence status (Abidin and Rasiah 2009; Pak 2011). If Malaysia is to move out of the middle-income trap and into higher value-added activities, training and skills development to enhance its human resource capabilities is essential (Abidin and Rasiah 2009).

Furthermore, Malaysia also focused on removing barriers to startups and risk-taking in moving Malaysia along the road to recovery and high-growth entrepreneurship (Ortmans 2011). The effort has already achieved some results, as Malaysia's entrepreneurialism is ranked 34th out of 104 economies in the Legatum's Entrepreneurship and Opportunity sub-index and 21st among 183 economies in the World Bank's Doing Business index (Ortmans 2011).

The Philippines

In 2010, a new government led by Aquino was elected and brings new hope to the country. Because of the corruption allegations against his two predecessors, Aquino's first step was to install leaders who are ethical, honest, and true public servants. He pledged not only to 'set the example' himself but also to hold similarly high standards for those who join the government (CIA 2012). As a result, investors have confidence in the Philippines' future economy and believed the new government will focus on government transparency, regulation of critical utilities such as fuel, water and energy, and poverty alleviation (ING 2010).

The Philippine government has set its Development Plan with a particular focus on inclusive growth, with key measures of infrastructure investment, governance reform, investments in education and health, and support for the poor (Singh 2011). Its medium-term development plan (2011–2016) aims toward inclusive growth that is rapid, sustainable, job-creating, and poverty-reducing (OECD 2012a). Special attention is paid to infrastructure development, including the development of public–private partnerships schemes, governance, human development, and the strengthening of public finance and financial institutions. Reducing poverty and inequality are other important priorities. Similarly, enhancing the business environment, especially for small and medium enterprises, and improving their productivity are critical for inclusive growth. In addition, the importance of sustainable agriculture and fisheries is also highlighted by the medium-term development plan. Furthermore, equitable access to basic social services, such as education, health care and housing, stronger social safety nets, the environment and natural resources, and peace and security are also included in the medium-term development plan.

Another area of the government's focus is to increase funding for infrastructure development and to attract more private participation by establishing an infrastructure fund and enhancing its availability through public–private partnership. The success of this aim should help accumulate more process capital.

The Philippine government also emphasizes improving the access to and the quality of basic education, technical education, and vocational training. Particularly, stronger Technical Education and Vocational Training (TEVT) is critical in the Philippines to help its industries move up in the value chain (OECD 2012b). Therefore, National Competency-Based Teacher Standards were implemented to strengthen the assessment of teacher's quality, a School Improvement Program to bolster educational capacity and to enhance the independence of school management in exchange for stronger accountability (OECD 2012a). Reforming the tax system to enhance tax collection and widen the tax base also helps strengthen the economy.

The Philippines is also working to reduce the government deficit from 3.9 % of GDP to 2 % of GDP by 2013 (CIA 2012).

Thailand

There is a prevailing mentality in Thailand that the global economy will recover over the next few years and thereafter competition will intensify. Therefore, Thailand should take the opportunity during the next few years to strengthen its productivity and competitiveness, so that when demand resumes, they can act quickly. As a result, Thailand continues its structural, financial and corporate sector reforms. Proposed measures include strengthening the intra-regional trade and investment, embarking continuous structural reforms, abiding by the international rules to raise the level of investment, enhancing governance systems through information technology, fostering value-added industries, and encouraging green management.

After the crisis, there is a general awareness in Thailand that for medium-term recovery, it has to go through intra-regional trade and investments rather than depending solely on the crisis-hit western countries. The potential could come from emerging markets around the world and particularly China, India and a few other ASEAN countries with sizable domestic consumption (Chirathivat and Mallikamas 2010). Therefore, its multilateral free trade agreements between ASEAN and other countries have increased significantly. Future potential growth of the region through trade and investment suggests that the demand for final goods and services in the region could increase much more than the present level (Chirathivat and Mallikamas 2010).

As Thailand continued its structural reforms, its second Strategic Plan was for the Thai Public Sector Development (2008–2012); that is, the public sector needs to enhance the quality of its services (Verghis and Bhaopichitr 2008). Under the new framework, each ministry will have to improve and integrate the 4-year plan in the form of a rolling plan. The 4-year plan will be revised each year so that it is more forward looking and flexible to change. This rolling plan will also be consistent to the medium-term expenditure framework which stipulates that sector ministries can budget annually with projected resource needs for three years into the future (Verghis and Bhaopichitr 2008).

The Thai government has also noticed a slowly growing investment and was planning on raising the levels of investment as well as productivity. As a result, Thailand continues to reduce import tariff rates for various products. To attract more investments, the Bank of Thailand also fully implements the new international standard, commonly known as Basel II, to extend its coverage of the reserve requirement by accounting for market and operational risk in addition to credit risk. The implementation of the Basel II will increase the bank's creditability and transparency. It will also force local banks to substantially upgrade their information technology and risk-management systems.

Following suit, the Stock Exchange of Thailand has installed a new trading system to facilitate future growth. This new system, which matches with those used by leading global stock market, can accommodate higher trade volumes and new products and support the planned ASEAN Linkage project. The Customs Department also significantly extended the application of e-Customs aiming to speed up customs procedures, enhance the transparency of these processes, and reduce the transaction costs incurred to exporters. With these mechanisms in place, risk information is more widely shared among export credit agencies in Asia. The Thai Export Import Bank together with export credit agencies in Australia, Indonesia, Japan, South Korea, Malaysia, the Philippines, Hong Kong, and Taiwan agreed to enhance information sharing, so that exporters can better cope with escalated risks and track delayed payments (Verghis and Bhaopichitr 2008).

Thailand is also ambitious in developing the country into a creative industries hub of ASEAN and has a goal to increase the contribution of the creative industries from 12 to 20 % of its GDP by 2012, based on Creative Economy 2010 report.

Lastly, green management is also on the agenda, as the Thai government has exempted import duties of many natural gas-related tools and equipment such as bio-fuel conversion kits, natural gas containers, and chasses (Verghis and Bhaopichitr 2008). Yet, achieving the above stated goals will require serious effort from all stakeholders, including the government, the private sector, and academia. These improvements take time and concerted effort. One promising sign is that Thailand is the first ASEAN country to develop carbon labels, which help its economy to move towards a low carbon trend. The new Carbon Footprint Label is currently being tested by a number of companies, including Thai Airlines International, the first airline in the world that calculates the carbon footprint of its in-flight meals (OECD 2011).

Challenges

After the 2008 global financial crisis, most ASEAN countries mapped their mid-term development plan to continue the required structural reforms for building a more resilient economy. While the challenges that each country faces may vary, human capital development has been identified as a key policy area in all the development plans for all four countries (OECD 2012b). This reflects the need for manpower with ever increasing skills amid rapid transformation of economic structures. To develop more skill- and knowledge-intensive industries and strengthen their competitiveness in the medium to long term, a flexible education system that is responsive to industry needs is required. Although the region has been relatively successful in raising school enrollment rates, their education systems need to become more outcome-oriented to guarantee a high-quality labor force. In addition, most ASEAN countries need to widen their tax bases and phase out unnecessary tax expenditures (OECD 2012b). The following section reports specific challenges each country may encounter.

Indonesia

After the financial crisis, the Indonesian government faces the ongoing challenge of improving Indonesia's infrastructure to remove impediments to growth. In addition, Indonesia also struggles with poverty and unemployment, corruption, a complex regulatory environment, and unequal resource distribution among regions. Mainly based on OECD (2010) suggestions (data source is cited, if otherwise), they include:

1. Indonesia would benefit from softening foreign direct investment barriers and public spending should be shifted toward growth-enhancing outlays.
2. Indonesia needs a well-designed regulatory framework and a healthy business environment to accelerate infrastructure development. Formally evaluating their operations at regular intervals will also benefited Indonesia's economic development.
3. Tax collection could be made more effective and higher revenues collected through continuous improvement in governance and enforcement.
4. Although anti-corruption legislation was implemented and the legal framework was improved, widespread corruption and red-tape bureaucracy continue to restrain the country's full potential for growth (Ziegenhain 2010). The pervasive corruption and weak judicial system also hamper the investment dynamism.
5. Attracting sufficient private investments will be challenging and will require establishing independent sectorial regulators and strengthening the powers of existing regulators. Although Indonesia's regulatory environment has improved, procedures for establishing and running a private enterprise are still time-consuming and costly due to lingering political interference.
6. The success of structural reforms will also rely on the introduction of effective compensation policies to support the real incomes of the poorest households and prevent an increase in poverty. The current labor code was originally introduced to protect formal-sector workers through generous severance payments and high minimum wages. However, such protection is a deterrent to hiring workers on formal contracts and encourages informality. Thus, Indonesia is characterized by a dual labor market, with a small formal market and a much larger informal sector, where workers lack social insurance. Extensive informality is detrimental to long-term growth by limiting training opportunities, capital accumulation and productivity gains. The coverage of formal social protection also needs to be increased.
7. About 70 % of the workforce in Indonesia is made up of informal workers with characteristics such as young, educated and dependent on their parents (Titiheruw et al. 2009), which means qualified human resources are not fully utilized.
8. Enrollment is particularly low in secondary education, suggesting the need to augment the transition from primary to higher levels of education by expanding the financial support.
9. In late 2010, increasing inflation, driven by higher and volatile food prices, posed an increasing challenge to economic policymakers and threatened to push millions of the near-poor below the poverty line.
10. Eliminating energy subsidies should be considered, as current energy subsidies fail to achieve their social objectives and entail significant economic, fiscal and environmental cost. The main challenge is to deal with the negative

side-effects of subsidy reduction. Communicating broadly the benefits of this reform, along with its distributional impact will be crucial. A phasing out of inefficient tax expenditure—in particular in the energy sector—will help expand government's fiscal base.

11. Environmental protection is a great concern, including deforestation; erosion of peat-lands; water pollution from industrial wastes, sewage; air pollution in urban areas; smoke and haze from forest fires. Indonesian government also needs to address the impact of climate change, the introduction of a carbon tax would help the country to efficiently reach its emissions-reduction targets (CIA 2012; OECD 2012).
12. Better coordination between national and local authorities and removing legal obstacles to land acquisition is also needed.

Malaysia

After the financial crisis, Malaysia needs to move to another stage of development to produce higher value-added products that can only be achieved in an innovation-driven economy dominated by technology-intensive operations (Abidin and Rasiah 2009). For example, the research and development (R&D) supporting organizations need to effectively facilitate the commercialization of R&D output from Malaysian universities. Furthermore, the financial crisis revealed fundamental weaknesses in Malaysia's economy, which provides an opportunity for the country to revise and restructure its approach towards longer term growth (Mei 2010). Mainly based on the report of Abidin and Rasiah (2009) and Mei (2010), the challenges Malaysia government likely to face include the following:

1. Fiscal deficit had been increased to 7.6 % of the GDP in 2009, compared with that of 4.8 % in 2008. Budget expansion may stimulate demand in the short run; nevertheless, the trailing effect is increasing deficit. To reduce the debt, government will have to cut spending or increase tax burden, this will generate crowding-out effects on consumption and investment. In addition, a larger fiscal deficit means the government needs to pay larger interest to the debt sources, instead of using the money for more productive purposes.
2. The increases in commodity prices have raised concerns about the possibility of high inflation once the global economy recovers.
3. Malaysia needs to create a favorable investment climate to attract more investors. To achieve this goal, the government should take appropriate steps to strengthen supply side factors, such as human capital through education and training, equipping labor force with efficient and required skills, and enhancing efficiency in production through technology.
4. To sustain growth in the longer term, there is a need to create an environment to encourage domestic consumption and investment with price stability. To boost domestic consumption, efforts must be put on increasing people's income.

5. Increasing people's income is in line with Malaysia's 2020 goal. To achieve the expected economic status, R&D activities are important elements for the country to step into new strategy of development. Yet, there is a scarce supply of engineers, R&D scientists, and technicians. In addition, the technological capability of universities graduates is still poor in the country and there is a prevailing reluctance of most qualified Malaysians to return home from foreign sites.
6. In addition, the percentage of Malaysia's gross R&D expenditure in GDP is relatively small in comparison with other Asian countries. The Malaysian government can launch a technological catch-up strategy to put the country on its 2020 growth path.
7. The Malaysian government should enhance the country's social security net, such as its healthcare system, education, benefits to elderly and disable groups, to reduce the need for precautionary savings.

The Philippines

The Philippines has made a notable recovery since mid-2009, driven mainly by strong export performance and has since pursued a series of legislative reforms to enhance the entrepreneurial environment and develop a stronger private sector to generate broader-based job growth. However, the economic development in Philippines is still slow. The challenges the new Aquino III government needs to face including the following (Singh 2011; CIA 2012; Heritage 2012; OECD 2012a):

1. The Philippines has a tight fiscal situation due to weak revenue generation. The weak tax collection, exacerbated by new tax breaks and incentives, has limited the government's ability to address major challenges.
2. Poor infrastructure, such as transportation and power facilities has inhibited private investment. As a result, the absence of entrepreneurial dynamism makes long-term economic development a difficult task.
3. Deeper institutional reforms are required in four interrelated areas: business freedom, investment freedom, property rights, and freedom from corruption. In addition, the government imposes formal and non-formal barriers to foreign investment.
4. The judicial system remains weak and vulnerable to political influence and corruption. Corruption and political instability result in pessimism in investment.
5. Poverty has worsened, mainly because of a high population growth rate and inequitable distribution of income. In the Philippines, poverty reduction remains an issue and leads to low domestic private investment.
6. Skill shortages are especially acute in several industries, notably engineering and business process outsourcing activities that require technical skills.

7. As a result of the financial crisis and subsequent fiscal stimulus measures, both the budget deficit and revenue have deteriorated. In 2009, the budget deficit increased to 3.7 %, although it fell back slightly to 3.5 % by 2010. Total revenue and taxes also dropped from 16.5 and 13.5 % of GDP respectively in 2007 to 13.4 and 12.1 % respectively by 2010. Low share of excise taxes on alcohol, tobacco and petroleum, inefficient and unnecessary tax incentives, and exemptions also narrow the tax base.
8. In the Philippines, environmental issues include uncontrolled deforestation especially in watershed areas; soil erosion; air and water pollution in major urban centers; coral reef degradation; and increasing pollution of coastal mangrove swamps that are important fish breeding grounds.

Thailand

After the financial crisis, Thailand needs to improve its productivity and investment climate to ensure its competitiveness in the near future. Experience from other Asian countries has shown that productivity improvements at the national level are achievable with concerted efforts by the private sector, government, and academia. The challenges Thailand will likely face in the near future include the following (Verghis and Bhaopichitr 2008; OECD 2011; CIA 2012; Heritage 2012):

1. A huge fiscal deficit of US$62.56 billion (Bt2.2 trillion) which would require the government to fulfill the gap.
2. Public investment levels in Thailand have been relatively low with its share in real GDP at only 5–6 % in the past few years. Efforts need to be made including streamlining the regulatory environment and improving public infrastructure. Such improvement will also boost investor confidence and investments in addition to inject funds directly into the economy.
3. Regulatory uncertainties and multiple bureaucratic processes are costly for firms and affect their investment decisions. The commonly complained factors include delays in tax refunds, uncertainties around the time taken to clear customs or obtain permits and certifications.
4. Lingering political instability is the major source which undermines the country's investment climate and economic potential. Corruption remains significant, both in the private and public sectors, and is often encountered in connection with government procurement, customs, and other business transactions.
5. Firms in Thailand need to raise their productivity and adaptability to the rapidly changing macroeconomic environment and the intensifying competition through greater product and service development, higher efficiency, and better risk management.
6. At the heart of productivity improvement is the quality of the country's human resource. However, shortages of required skills are constraining firm operations

as well as Thailand's transition toward a knowledge economy. In a 2007 business survey, more than two-fifths of firms indicated that the reasons for not engaging in more innovative activities were the lack of qualified personnel. More than 80 % of firms have expressed that indirect incentives from the government would help raise their innovative activities, while 70 % indicated that technical assistance by government agencies and organizations would help.
7. Political stability, clarity and continuity in policy directions, and greater public infrastructure investments are needed not only to help promote growth in the short-run, but also improve productivity for the longer-term growth.
8. Environmental protection is a concern in Thailand, including air pollution from vehicle emissions; water pollution from organic and factory wastes; deforestation; soil erosion; and wildlife populations threatened by illegal hunting.

Policy Implications

Unexpectedly, what started off as a sub-prime mortgage problem in the U.S. triggered the wide-spreading global financial crisis. Even the emerging economies with strong foreign exchange reserves and large domestic markets are not immune from the impact. This event clearly shows how interdependent and inter-connected the world economy has become.

The causes of this financial crisis are multifaceted. They include high risk financial products, undisclosed conflicts of interest, and failure of regulation and the credit rating agencies. The sovereignty debt problem broke out in the European Union region added more complex dimensions to this crisis. Furthermore, fragile financial system, relax risk management, and weak national governance augmented the problems. It is a linking system breakdown that failed to withhold the impact of sudden financial shock.

Behind such statistics as the percentage GDP growth decrease and export volume decrease are the hidden factors of people, systems, governance, market dynamics, and the global interdependence that caused this global financial catastrophe. National intellectual capital (NIC) represents a major part of national intangible assets. Research results reported in this booklet provide valuable information for policy makers to look back on the national intangibles before the crisis, observe their co-development with the GDP during and after the crisis, and then draw lessons from it.

By investigating the economic development and NIC development spanning 2005–2010 at the same time, we have been able to connect the co-evolution of tangibles and intangibles for the reported four countries. Implications that can be drawn from our research findings are as follows:

First, NIC development goes together with the economic development and should be regarded as an enhancer of economic growth. The co-development of NIC and GDP with a high positive correlation (Fig. 3.7) indicates that the higher the NIC, the higher the GDP. This means that intangible intellectual capital development accompanies GDP growth for the 48 countries as a whole. Yet, Figs. 3.8–3.12 reveal that GDP growth is relatively flat in these four countries, even though there is good NIC improvement. These observations lead to the question "Why didn't NIC improvement accompany GDP growth as it did in other advanced countries?" The answer may lie in the value adding of the intangibles. This implication is in line with Malaysia's acknowledgement that it should move toward high-value, high-tech manufacturing, skill training, and high-income status. Therefore, attending to the development of NIC should be a strategic issue for nations intended to prosper in the knowledge economy.

Second, sound financial systems help withstand external financial shock. The four Southeast Asian countries presented in this volume weathered the 2008 global financial crisis well, mainly because of their sound financial systems reformed after the 1997 Asian financial crisis. Central banks of these four countries have also been accredited with their timely and proper intervening measures to stabilize the financial order. Objective statistics indicate that real GDP growth and consumer price inflation of these four countries were indeed fluctuated with the financial crisis (Figs. 2.1 and 2.4). After the crisis, these two indicators had either resumed or became better than their 2005 statuses. In 2010, the general government debt of Indonesia and the Philippines even decreased comparing to their 2005 status, and that of Malaysia and Thailand increased a little only (Fig. 2.2). Unemployment rate of the four countries not only was unaffected by the financial crisis but also improved, comparing 2010 with 2005 status (Fig. 2.3).

Third, always maintaining adequate amounts of foreign exchange reserves can safeguard a nation from sudden economic shock. As reported, all the four countries have been able to escape from the financial crisis much faster than a lot of countries. The financial stimulus plans did work with quick results, in spite all four countries were hard hit by the crisis due to sudden and sharp export decline and foreign capitals outflows. In addition to the laudable prompt actions of these governments and the growing demand of Asian countries, strong international reserve of these four countries has a lot to do with their fast and successful recovery. This implies that always maintaining comfortable amount of international reserves can safeguard a nation from sudden economic shock. This message is especially meaningful for those EU countries that are still in financial trouble in 2012.

Fourth, searching for a balance between export encouragement and domestic markets expansion is an important task. From our reports, the main reason that these countries were dragged into this 2008 global financial turmoil is not because of the impact of the first wave financial troubles that started in the western countries; rather it was because of the subsequent sudden foreign investment withdrawal and sharp drop of export demands. With the experience of this crisis, these governments are working on strengthening the domestic markets and reducing export reliance, especially Malaysia and Thailand who are more export-dependent. Nevertheless, export is still an important source of national growth, as it brings prosperity and more advanced technologies. However, remaining the same economic development pattern without policy change may be unsustainable. Therefore, searching for a balance between export encouragement and domestic market expansion is a feasible solution to resist future financial shock.

Fifth, efficient disbursement of assigned stimulus money is even more important than the stimulus plans. In these four countries, people in greater need of assistance during the financial crisis are generally populated at the remote rural areas where communication media is relatively inefficient. From our report, relevant governments have acknowledged their own unique situation and adopt proactive measures to promote speedier stimulus disbursement in pulling its people out of troubles. For instance, Malaysia has established a Project Management Unit to monitor the progress of its stimulus package. Thai government also mapped out clear goals and distribution channels of implementing short-term rescue as well as medium-term development details for scheduled monitoring.

Sixth, utilizing stimulus packages to launch structural reforms for economic transformation is an effective strategy. Each country has its own historical background and political problems that may hamper necessary reforms in good times. Yet in difficult times, political parties are more likely to collaborate for the greatest benefits of the country. In addition, extra resources enable more deep-rooted reforms that require resources and commitment. From our literature review, these four countries have put their mid-term and long-term goals in sight when planning for the stimulus packages. For example, based on the Medium Term Development Plan, the Indonesian government is shifting attention in the design of its social-protection programs from crisis mitigation to strengthening support for vulnerable households to help them pull themselves out of poverty and equip the poor with the means to prevent a long-lasting fall into poverty. Malaysia is attempting to achieve high-income status by 2020 and to move farther up the value-added production chain by calling for more R&D investment and upgrading its human resources for technology capability.

Seventh, developing renewal capital should generate high value for Malaysia and Thailand. Figure 3.12 manifests that the co-development pattern of renewal capital and GDP growth for Malaysia and Thailand is by no means flat. They are the two most unique development paths presented in this volume with promising indications. These two countries should deepen their past efforts in renewal and strategize for a more effective future development. In addition, when examining Figs. 3.12 and 3.13b long-term NIC together, it is also clear that the almost vertical human capital growth of these two countries did not accompany with renewal capital increase, implying the added-value of human capital improvement is limited. Generally, renewal capital relies on good human capital. As Malaysia aspires to move farther up the value-added production chain, this is definitely the area that the country should pay more attention.

Eighth, establishing sound safety nets together with a high growth and export-dependent national development strategy is essential in building a more resilient economy. During this financial crisis, a prevalent awareness among these four countries is reducing export dependence and expanding domestic markets. Low dependence on export can indeed insulate the country from external impact, yet it also slows down national growth, as the case of the Philippines. Foreign direct investment and production for export help upgrade skills and technology in emerging countries and are an important source of national growth. That is, there is nothing wrong with the export-dependent model, as long as the country has set up good safety nets. Specifically, countries pursue growth model through export need to have a comfortable level of international reserves, establish resilient financial systems with easy access to transparent information, have social protection system that can efficiently reach the poorest households any time, and have good governance systems. With sound safety nets in place, export-dependent economies like Hong Kong, Korea, Singapore, and Taiwan all rebounded swiftly after hard hit by this global financial crisis.

Ninth, pursuing political stability is the formula for a nation's continuous growth. Although still low in GDP, Indonesia's economic performance during 2005–2010 is outstanding among these four countries. One of the key reasons may be attributed to the step down of its long-standing authoritarian ruler in 1998. Ever since, the crackdown on corruption and the encouragement of much-needed foreign investment have helped the country make its way to the path of growth. From its capacity in weathering through this financial crisis and various indicators introduced in this report, Indonesia should be able to catch up with the Philippines very soon. On the other hand, the Philippines used to be a prosperous society decades ago, unfortunately continuous corruption scandals have disrupted the political stability of the country and hamper its national growth. More recently, the political dispute in Thailand during this financial crisis also delayed the announcement of the stimulus package. In the keener global competition, citizen's well-being will be sacrificed by the country's internal political strife which should be avoided.

Tenth, establishing regional supporting system is an effective way to combat financial crisis. The current crisis is more severe than past ones because more individuals, financial institutions and countries were involved. Hence, resolution needs the coordinated international efforts for a fundamental restructuring. Global crisis handling by the G20 economies have demonstrated the effectiveness of working collectively. For example, G20 members have re-emphasized the Non-Protectionist Agreement by maintaining an open trade and investment regime. In addition, their economies have also agreed to step up trade financing to encourage the growth of international trade. Policy coordination among economies is a crucial step in overcoming the negative impact of a global crisis, as mutual interest must be prioritized and each economy must strive to avoid seeking benefits for one country at the expense of others (Adriyanto 2009). A regional and global economic cooperation to monitor the development of economic and financial sector through early warning system is also critical to ensure timely handling of future crisis. The collaboration among ASEAN countries in this financial crisis also proves the value of regional supporting system. In regards to this ever increasing vulnerability, world economies must collaborate not only to ensure an integrated and effective solution towards global crisis but also to establish an effective global surveillance and monitoring system (Adriyanto 2009).

Concluding Remarks and Emerging Insights

This global financial crisis came with an unexpected speed and negative effects, yet the governments of the four countries have navigated their countries through the crisis well. The initial notion that emerging economies and countries with strong foreign exchange reserves could be decoupled from the financial crisis has been proven wrong. All four countries were still hit with sharp drops in export demand and the outflows of foreign capitals. With the experience of the 1997 Asian financial crisis and the ensuing reforms, these four countries were in a better financial position at the inception of the 2008 global financial crisis. In addition, they all had comfortable international reserves at their discretion to increase spending and boost consumer demand, thus making them more resilient to this crisis. The recovery of these four Southeast Asian countries is fast, which began to show at the last quarter of 2009.

In early 2011, World Economic Forum reported that worldwide recovery appeared fairly certain, with economic growth for 2011 and 2012 projected by the IMF at 4.3 and 4.5 %, respectively. In the first quarter of 2012, global growth was 3.6 %. For Asia, growth was pulled up by a greater-than-anticipated rebound in industrial production, spurred by the restart of supply chains disrupted by the Thai floods in late 2011, and stronger-than-expected domestic demand in Japan after the earthquake. However, in the second quarter of 2012, growth momentum has slowed in various emerging market economies, notably Brazil, China, and India, partly reflecting a weaker external environment. Overall, global growth is projected to moderate to 3.5 % in 2012 and 3.9 % in 2013 and growth in emerging and developing economies will moderate to 5.6 % in 2012 and 5.9 % in 2013. IMF (2012) suggests that policymakers in emerging and developing economies should stand ready to adjust policies, given spillovers from weaker advanced economy prospects, slowing export growth and volatile capital flows.

As a recap, to counter worsening economic conditions worldwide, a total of US$2 trillion in stimulus packages, amounting to approximately 3 % of the world gross domestic product, has been allocated (some of the packages include measures that extend into subsequent years), an amount that exceeds the call by the IMF for fiscal stimulus totaling 2 % of the global GDP. IMF also estimated that as of January 2009, the U.S. fiscal stimulus packages as a percentage of the GDP in 2009 would amount to 1.9 %, for the Euro area 0.9 %, for Japan 1.4 %, for Asia excluding Japan 1.5 %, and for the rest of the G-20 countries 1.1 % (Nanto 2009).

The 2008 global financial crisis has provided an excellent opportunity for nations to assess the policy responses and to discuss the options for restoring economic growth in reducing the social impact. Presumably, national leaders should have learned some valuable lessons from this financial crisis and will have better foresight to avoid being trapped in similar situations again. However, such confidence comes from continuously reexamining the adequacy of national strategies, policies and governance in coping with the increasingly interconnected and rapidly changing global economic environment.

As the center of global economic activities will gradually shift from the west to Asia in the near future, ASEAN countries have great opportunities to advance their economies if their infrastructure, systems and NIC development are ready for the challenge. To fully take advantage of this, continuous reforms to strengthen their economic and social fundamentals are required. Yet, the path of structural reforms is long and laborious. This volume has provided some guidelines in section Challenges for the policy makers to consider.

In terms of future NIC development, our other study of the top ten NIC ranking countries reveals that the interplay among the four capitals—human capital, market capital, process capital, and renewal capital—resulted in the best synergic prospect for GDP growth. When their weaker capital (process capital) interacts with stronger capital (market capital), both effects on the GDP are enhanced (Lin 2011). Such findings agree with the national growth of Malaysia with its relatively balanced NIC development.

At the completion of reporting the impact of the financial crisis on these four Southeast Asian countries from a NIC perspective, we have a strong feeling that national success is a capability that accumulates over time; it does not come within a short period of time or from overnight wealth. National economic development is built upon the well-coordinated systems of tangibles and intangible, including money, real assets, human capital, market capital, process capital, and renewal capital systems described in this booklet. As the very origin of the financial crisis—people, systems, governance, market dynamics, and the global interdependence—they are also the keys to the economic recovery in any place and country. It is a fundamental function of government to create and maintain both tangible and intangible infrastructure under which the economic, social and cultural life of the citizens can prosper. Looking back at the 2008 global financial crisis through the lens of NIC provides a different perspective for policy makers to ponder on.

Appendix 1
Summary of the Main Stimulus Packages of the Four Southeast Asian Countries

C. Y.-Y. Lin et al., *National Intellectual Capital and the Financial Crisis in Indonesia, Malaysia, The Philippines, and Thailand*, SpringerBriefs in Economics,
DOI: 10.1007/978-1-4614-7943-7,

Country	Date	Amount	Item
Indonesia	Dec. 2008	#1 US$3.2 billion (IDR32 trillion)	An expansion of income tax relief for eight industries, subsidies for food, fertilizer and rice seeds
		#2 US$2.1 billion (IDR21 trillion)	Credit subsidies for business
		#2 US$1 brillion (IDR10 trillion)	Reserved as emergency assistance for various other businesses
			In addition to a 2 % corporate tax reduction, a further 5 % reduction is offered for companies listed on the stock exchange, so as to encourage medium-sized enterprises to list their shares on the stock exchange
	Jan. 2009	#3 US$7.6 billion (IDR73.3 trillion)—about 1.4 % of GDP, including the following 4 items:	
		#4 US$4.5 billion	Tax cut for companies, workers and individuals
		#4 US$0.5 billion	Diesel and electricity subsidies and loans for rural employment
		#4 US$1.3 billion	Infrastructure projects and empowerment program for people living in rural areas
		#4 US$1.4 billion	Tax subsidies and import duties exemption
		#3 US$31.5 million (IDR300 billion)	Ministry of Manpower and Transmigration allocated US$31.5 million (IDR300 billion) to vocational training. 45 % was used to deliver additional training to jobseekers and migrant workers as well as productivity enhancement. The remaining 55 % improved the physical infrastructure of training centers.
	Feb. 24, 2009	#1 US$200 million (IDR2 trillion)	Due to Indonesian parliamentary intervention, the total amount of the package was increased by US$200 million

(continued)

(continued)

Country	Date	Amount	Item
Malaysia	Nov. 2008	#5 US$1.9 billion (MYR7 billion) or 1.04 % GDP	43 % for infrastructure to ensure the well-being of citizens, develope quality human capital, and strengthen national resilience
	Mar. 2009	#5 #6 US$16.2 billion (MYR 60 billion), or 9 % of GDP (two packages total US$18.1 billion, or 10.4 % GDP)	US$1.4 billion (MYR5 billion) in 2009, US$1.4 billion (MYR5 billion) in 2010 out of US$16.2 billion (MYR60 billion). The balance is in the form of guarantees, tax deductions and allocations to the National Sovereign Fund. 48 % (US$6.8 billion (MYR 25 billion)) is directed towards assisting the private sector as bank guarantees for SMEs. 32 % is allocated to infrastructure for maintenance rather than new spending on public facilities. 17 % for food, toll and fuel subsidies to support for low-cost housing and for retrenched workers. The remaining 3 % for reducing unemployment and increasing job and training opportunities. The stimulus package comprised US$4.9 billion (MYR15 billion) in direct fiscal stimulus and US$812.6 million (MYR3 billion) in tax incentives. The remaining US$11.4 billion (MYR42 billion) are in the form of guaranteed funds, equity interests and private finance initiatives and off-budget initiatives.
The Philippines	2009	#7 #8 US$7 billion (PHP330 billion) or 4 % GDP Economic Resiliency Plan (ERP)	The US$7 billion (PHP330 billion) Economic Resiliency Plan (ERP) includes the following: •US$3.3 billion (PHP160 billion) is the increase in the 2009 budget compared to the 2008 budget. This funds small, community-level infrastructure projects and social protection measures •US$834 million (PHP40 billion) is the combined tax cuts for low and middle income earners and the scheduled cut in corporate income taxes as provided in the revised value added tax law •US$2.1 billion (PHP100 billion) is outside the budget. Part of the fund will be provided by government financial institutions and social security institutions to finance large infrastructure projects •US$625 million (PHP30 billion) is the additional benefits to members by social security institutions. This will be taken from the gap between contributions and claims/benefits

(continued)

(continued)

Country	Date	Amount	Item
	FY2009	#7 US$214 million (PHP10.07 billion)	An Economic Stimulus Fund was created to supplement regular budget programs of several national government agencies: including scholarships, training programs, reintegration programs for displaced overseas Filipino workers, construction of school buildings, medical assistance to remote areas, food production, protection of forests, marine, and watershed areas and recycling of agriculture waste products
	Oct. 11, 2011	#9 US$1.66 billion (PHP 72 billion)	Government's additional spending this year includes US$149 million (PHP6.5 billion) for local infrastructure and poverty alleviation and US$230 million (PHP10 billion) to relocate squatters affected by floods and landslides Another US$126 million (PHP5.5 billion) will be spent on national infrastructure projects and US$146 million (PHP6.3 billion) to upgrade two of metropolitan Manila's light rail lines
Thailand	Mar. 2008	#10 US$1.14 billion (THB40 billion, 0.4 % GDP)	Reducing taxes. Higher deductible for personal income taxes, a reduction in corporate income tax rates, increased tax deduction on machines and equipment, and reduced property sales transaction fees
	Apr. 2008	#10 US$12.7 billion (THB445.8 billion)	Assist low income households through grant transfers, reduction in debt for farmers, and increasing extension of micro-credit to the grass root level
	Jul. 2008	US$1.42 billion (THB50 billion)	Six measures for six months, from subsidy of gasoline, water, and electricity to bus and train services
	Oct. 2008	US$27 billion (THB950 billion)	Injection of liquidity into the credit market, support the tourism industry, instill confidence in insurance market, and prevent capital outflows
	Jan. 2009	#11 US$3.27 billion (THB115 billion)	Focusing on consumption rather than investment and targeting 7 groups of people: farmers, low income earners, parents, SMEs, community-based enterprises, senior citizens, and self employed
	Jan. 20, 2009 2nd stimulus package	#11 US$1.42 billion (THB50 billion) tax reduction	Targeting 4 groups: property business, SMEs, community enterprises, and tourism business
		#11 Quasi-fiscal policy	To revitalize the economy and develop infrastructure, the government has announced its plan to borrow US$5.7 billion (THB200 billion) from local banks and US$2 billion (THB70 billion) from World Bank, Asian Development Bank and Japan International Cooperation Agency

(continued)

(continued)

Country	Date	Amount	Item
		#11 US$40.7 billion (1.43 trillion baht)	The off-budget US$40.7 billion (1.43 trillion baht) covered 3-year SP2 stimulus package (2010–2012) (SP2 consists of US$31.6 billion (THB1.11 trillion) government projects and US$9.1 billion (THB321 billion) state-owned enterprise investment projects)

#1. Ziegenhain P (2010) Indonesia country report. In: Stiftung B (ed) Managing the crisis. A comparative assessment of economic Governance in 14 economies. Bertelsmann Stiftung, Gütersloh

#2. The Jakarta Post (2008) Editorial: budget geared for crisis. Retrieved from http://www.thejakartapost.com/news/2008/11/04/editorial-budget-geared-crisis.html

#3. International Labour Office (2010a) G20 country briefs: Indonesia's response to the crisis. G20 Meeting of Labour and Employment Ministers, Washington, D.C., 20–21 Apr 2010. Retrieved from http://www.ilo.org/public/libdoc/jobcrisis/download/g20_indonesia_countrybrief.pdf

#4. International Labour Office (2010b) G20 statistical update: Indonesia higher informal employment during the economic slowdown. G20 Meeting of Labour and Employment Ministers, Washington, D.C., 20–21 Apr 2010. Retrieved from http://www.dol.gov/ilab/media/events/G20_ministersmeeting/G20-Indonesia-stats.pdf

#5. Abidin MZ, Rasiah R (2009b) The global financial crisis and the Malaysian economy: impact and responses. UNDP, Malaysia. Retrieved from http://www.undp.org.my/uploads/undp%>20report%20-the%20global%20financial%20crisis%20and%20the%20malaysian%20economy.pdf

#6. Mah-Hui ML, Khoon GS (2010) The impact of the global financial crisis: the case of Malaysia. Third World Network Global Economy Series. Retrieved from http://www.twnside.org.sg/title2/ge/ge26.pdf

#7. Balisacan A, Piza S, Mapa D, Santos CA, Odra D (2010b) The Philippine economy and poverty during the global economic crisis. The Philippine Rev Econ (47.1):1–37. Retrieved from http://pre.econ.upd.edu.ph/index.php/pre/article/view/644/3

#8. Yap JT, Reyes CM, Cuenca JS (2009b) Impact of global financial and economic crisis on the Philippines. Philippine Institute for Development Studies, Discussion Paper Series No. 2009-30. Retrieved from http://www.unicef.org/socialpolicy/files/Impact_of_the_Global_Finanical_and_Economic_Crisis_on_the_Philippines.pdf

#9. Boston.com (2011) Philippines unveils $1.6 billion stimulus package. Retrieved from http://www.boston.com/business/articles/2011/10/12/philippines_unveils_16_billion_stimulus_package/, 12 Oct 2011

#10. Verghis MA, Bhaopichitr K (2008b) Thailand economic monitor. World Bank Office, Bangkok. Retrieved from http://siteresources.worldbank.org/INTTHAILAND/Resources/Economic-Monitor/2008april_tem.pdf

#11. Chirathivat S, Mallikamas S (2010b) Thailand's economic performance and responses to the global crisis. A paper presented at the ACAES Conference "Asia after the Crisis" jointly organized with Doshisha University, 5–6 March 2010, Kyoto. Retrieved from http://ccas.doshisha.ac.jp/eng/Econference/econfpdf/26th%20Conference%20of%20the%20American%20Committee%20for%20Asian%20Economic%20Studies/Suthiphand.pdf

Appendix 2
Important Meetings Held by World Leaders to Address the 2008 Global Financial Crisis

Date	Place	Participants
June 18–19, 2012	Los Cabos, Mexico	G20
June 17, 2012	Los Cabos, Mexico	G7 Finance Ministers
March 1–2, 2012	Brussels	European Council
January 30, 2012	Brussels	Informal meeting of members of the European Council
December 8–9, 2011	Brussels	European Council
November 12–13, 2011	Honolulu, USA	19th APEC Economic Leaders' meeting
November 3–4, 2011	Cannes, France	G20
October 23, 2011	Brussels	European Council
September 10, 2011	Marseille	G8 Deauville partnership finance ministers
September 9–10, 2011	Marseille	G7 finance ministers and central bank governors
July 21, 2011	Brussels	Meeting of heads of state or government of the Euro area
June 23–24, 2011	Brussels	European Council
March 24–25, 2011	Brussels	European Council
March 17, 2011	Japan	G7 finance ministers telephone conference
March 11, 2011	Brussels	Extraordinary European Council
February 4, 2011	Brussels	European Council
December 16–17, 2010	Brussels	European Council
November 21, 2010	Ireland	G7 finance ministers
November 13–14, 2010	Yokohama, Japan	18th APEC Economic Leaders' meeting
November 11–12, 2010	Seoul, Korea	G20
October 28–29, 2010	Brussels	European Council
October 8, 2010	Washington DC	G7 finance ministers and central bank governors
September 16, 2010	Brussels	European Council
June 26–27, 2010	Toronto, Canada	G20
June 17, 2010	Brussels	European Council

(continued)

C. Y.-Y. Lin et al., *National Intellectual Capital and the Financial Crisis in Indonesia, Malaysia, The Philippines, and Thailand*, SpringerBriefs in Economics, DOI: 10.1007/978-1-4614-7943-7,

(continued)

Date	Place	Participants
March 25–26, 2010	Brussels	European Council
February 11, 2010	Brussels	Informal meeting of heads of state or government of the European Union
February 5–6, 2010	Iqaluit, Nunavut, Canada	G7 finance ministers and central bank governors
December 10–11, 2009	Brussels	European Council
November 19, 2009	Brussels	Informal meeting of heads of state or government of the European Union
November 14–15, 2009	Singapore	17th APEC Economic Leaders' meeting
October 29–30, 2009	Brussels	European Council
October 3, 2009	Istanbul, Turkey	G7 finance ministers and central bank governors
September 24–25, 2009	Pittsburgh, USA	G20
September 17, 2009	Brussels	Informal meeting of heads of state or government of the European Union
June 18–19, 2009	Brussels	European Council
June 12–13, 2009	Lecce, Italy	G8 finance ministers
April 24, 2009	Washington DC	G7 finance ministers and central bank governors
April 2, 2009	G20 London Summit United Kingdom	G20
March 19–20, 2009	Brussels	European Council
February 2009	Rome	G7 finance ministers and central bank governors
December 11–12, 2008	Brussels	European Council
November 2008	G20 APEC Peru	G20
November 22–23, 2008	Lima, Peru	16th APEC Economic Leaders' Meeting
November 14–15, 2008	Washington D.C., USA	G7
October 15–16, 2008	Brussels	European Council
October 10, 2008	Washington, DC	G7 Finance Ministers
September 1, 2008	Brussels	Extraordinary European Council
July 7–9, 2008	Tokyo	34th G8 Summit
June 19–20, 2008	Brussels	European Council
June 13–14, 2008	Osaka	G8 Finance Ministers meeting
March 13–14, 2008	Brussels	European Council
February 9, 2008	Tokyo	G7 Finance Ministers and Central Bank Governors meeting

For further information
http://g20mexico.org/en/g20/previous-leaders-summits
http://www.98.utoronto.ca/finance/index.htm
http://www.european-council.europa.eu/council-meetings/conclusions
http://www.apec.org/
http://video.consilium.europa.eu/ecofin/

Appendix 3
Indicators in Each Type of Capital

Human capital index	*Market capital index*
1. Skilled labor*	1. Corporate tax*
2. Employee training*	2. Cross-border venture*
3. Literacy rate	3. Openness of culture*
4. Higher education enrollment	4. Globalization*
5. Pupil-teacher ratio	5. Transparency*
6. Internet subscribers	6. Image of country*
7. Public expenditure on education	7. Exports of goods
Process capital index	*Renewal capital index*
1. Business competition environment*	1. Business R&D spending
2. Government efficiency*	2. Basic research*
3. Intellectual property rights protection*	3. R&D spending/GDP
4. Capital availability*	4. R&D researchers
5. Computers in use per capita	5. Cooperation between universities and enterprises*
6. Convenience of establishing new firms*	6. Scientific articles
7. Mobile phone subscribers	7. Patents per capita (USPTO + EPO)

Remarks
1. Financial capital is the logarithm of GDP per capita adjusted by purchasing power parity.
2. Indicators marked with an asterisk are rated qualitatively using a scale of 1–10.
3. Indicators with objective numbers are transformed to 1–10 scores, by calculating the ratio to the highest number in that indicator and then multiply 10.
4. Readers can refer to the book *National Intellectual Capital: A Comparison of 40 Countries* for model validation details (www.nic40.org)

C. Y.-Y. Lin et al., *National Intellectual Capital and the Financial Crisis in Indonesia, Malaysia, The Philippines, and Thailand*, SpringerBriefs in Economics, DOI: 10.1007/978-1-4614-7943-7, © The Author(s) 2014

Appendix 4
Definition of the 29 Indicators

Indicators	Definition
Human capital	
Skilled labor*	Whether skilled labor is readily available
Employee training*	Whether employee training is a high propriety in companies
Literacy rate	Adult (over 15 years) literacy rate as a percentage of population
Higher education enrollment	Percentage of population that has attained at least tertiary education
Pupil-teacher ratio	Ratio of teaching staff to students
Internet subscribers	Number of internet users per 1000 people
Public expenditure on education	Total public expenditure on education (percentage of GDP)
Market Capital	
Corporate tax encouragement*	Whether corporate taxes encourage entrepreneurial activity
Cross-border venture*	Whether international transactions can be freely negotiated with foreign partners
Openness to foreign culture*	Whether the national culture is open to foreign culture ideas
Attitudes toward globalization*	Whether attitudes toward globalization are generally positive in a given society
Transparency*	Whether transparency of government policy is satisfactory
Country image*	Whether the image abroad of a given country encourages business development
Exports of goods	Exports of goods (Percentage of GDP)
Process Capital	
Business competition environment*	Whether competition legislation is efficient in preventing unfair competition
Government efficiency*	Whether government bureaucracy hinders business activity
Intellectual property rights protection*	Whether intellectual property rights are adequately enforced
Capital availability*	Whether cost of capital encourages business development
Computers in use per capita	Number of computers per 1000 people
Convenience of establishing new firms*	Whether creation of firms is supported by legislation
Mobile phone subscribers	Number of subscribers per 1000 inhabitants

(continued)

C. Y.-Y. Lin et al., *National Intellectual Capital and the Financial Crisis in Indonesia, Malaysia, The Philippines, and Thailand*, SpringerBriefs in Economics,
DOI: 10.1007/978-1-4614-7943-7,

(continued)

Indicators	Definition
Renewal Capital	
Business R&D spending	Business expenditure on R&D (per capita)
Basic research*	Whether basic research enhances long-term economic development
R&D spending/GDP	Total expenditure on R&D (percentage of GDP)
R&D researchers	Total R&D personnel nationwide per capita (Full-time work equivalent per 1000 people)
Cooperation between universities and enterprises*	Whether knowledge transfer is highly developed between universities and companies
Scientific articles	Scientific articles published by origin of author (per capita)
Patents per capita (USPTO + EPO)	USPTO and EPO total patents granted (per capita)
Financial Capital	
GDP per capita (PPP) (From IMF)	Gross domestic product based on purchasing-power-parity (PPP) per capita

Appendix 5
48 Countries by Cluster and by Continent

This booklet series covers a total of 48 countries in 11 country clusters. China, Brazil and South Africa are grouped twice to maintain cluster completeness. China is in both the Greater China region and the BRICKS region, Brazil is in both the BRICKS region and the Latin American region, and South Africa is in both the BRICKS region and in Cluster 5.

The eleven country clusters:

1. Portugal, Italy, Greece, Spain
2. Greater China region (China, Hong Kong, Singapore, Taiwan)
3. Brazil, Russia, India, China, Korea, South Africa (BRICKS)
4. Indonesia, Malaysia, the Philippines, Thailand
5. Israel, Jordan, Turkey, South Africa
6. Bulgaria, Czech Republic, Hungary, Romania, Poland
7. Austria, Belgium, the Netherlands, Switzerland
8. France, Germany, Ireland, United Kingdom
9. Argentina, Brazil, Chile, Colombia, Mexico, Venezuela
10. Australia, Canada, Japan, New Zealand, USA
11. Denmark, Finland, Iceland, Norway, Sweden

48 countries by continent:

Europe—24 countries

Nordic Europe–Denmark, Finland, Iceland, Norway, and Sweden,
Western Europe–Austria, Belgium, France, Germany, Ireland, Netherlands, Switzerland, and UK.
Southern Europe–Greece, Italy, Portugal, and Spain
Eastern Europe–Russia

C. Y.-Y. Lin et al., *National Intellectual Capital and the Financial Crisis in Indonesia, Malaysia, The Philippines, and Thailand*, SpringerBriefs in Economics,
DOI: 10.1007/978-1-4614-7943-7, © The Author(s) 2014

East Central Europe–Bulgaria, Czech Republic, Hungary, Poland, Romania, Turkey

Americas—8 countries

North America–Canada, USA
Latin America–Argentina, Brazil, Chile, Colombia, Mexico, Venezuela

Australia—2 countries

Australia and New Zealand

Asia—13 countries

East Asia–China, Hong Kong, Japan, Korea, Taiwan
West Asia–Israel, Jordan
Southeast Asia–Indonesia, Malaysia, the Philippines, Singapore, Thailand
South Asia–India

Africa—1 country
South Africa

Appendix 6
National Intellectual Capital Scores and Ranking for 48 Countries (2005–2010)

C. Y.-Y. Lin et al., *National Intellectual Capital and the Financial Crisis in Indonesia, Malaysia, The Philippines, and Thailand*, SpringerBriefs in Economics, DOI: 10.1007/978-1-4614-7943-7, © The Author(s) 2014

2005–2010	Human capital		Market capital		Process capital		Renewal capital		Financial capital		NIC	
Mean	6.420		5.409		5.345		3.658		9.115		29.946	
SD	1.217		1.085		1.454		2.056		0.690		5.840	
Country	Score	Ranking	Score	Ranking	Score	Ranking	Score	Ranking	Score	Ranking	Score	Ranking
Argentina	5.370	36	3.340	47	3.038	47	1.413	45	8.755	34	21.916	45
Australia	7.205	15	6.199	12	6.938	9	4.927	16	9.695	11	34.964	13
Austria	7.229	14	6.203	11	6.982	8	5.296	12	9.708	10	35.418	11
Belgium	7.666	8	5.519	23	5.924	21	4.706	17	9.635	14	33.450	19
Brazil	4.757	44	4.589	38	3.076	46	1.753	36	8.481	40	22.656	42
Bulgaria	5.493	34	4.929	31	4.054	36	1.589	41	8.646	37	24.710	35
Canada	7.855	6	6.137	13	6.464	15	5.064	14	9.710	9	35.229	12
Chile	5.414	35	6.663	5	5.163	28	1.710	37	8.784	32	27.734	30
China	4.942	39	5.184	28	3.746	40	2.099	33	7.967	44	23.938	40
Colombia	4.941	40	4.677	36	3.951	37	1.435	44	8.348	42	23.352	41
Czech Republic	5.995	30	5.720	18	5.378	25	2.905	24	9.271	27	29.269	25
Denmark	8.545	1	6.662	6	7.642	1	6.587	6	9.665	13	39.101	3
Finland	7.601	9	6.232	10	7.399	3	7.755	3	9.606	17	38.593	4
France	6.956	20	4.141	45	5.730	22	4.500	20	9.585	18	30.912	23
Germany	6.761	23	5.630	19	6.489	14	5.796	9	9.612	16	34.287	17
Greece	5.986	31	4.216	43	4.113	35	2.168	32	9.440	23	25.923	31
Hong Kong	6.564	25	8.090	2	7.209	5	3.277	23	9.794	4	34.934	14
Hungary	6.674	24	4.836	32	5.095	29	2.301	29	9.046	29	27.952	29
Iceland	8.357	3	5.614	21	6.561	12	5.931	8	9.713	8	36.154	8
India	3.926	48	5.620	20	3.556	42	1.954	34	7.285	48	22.340	44
Indonesia	4.062	47	4.832	33	3.257	44	1.519	42	7.594	46	21.263	47
Ireland	7.145	16	6.816	3	6.711	11	4.101	21	9.768	5	34.541	16
Israel	8.040	4	5.954	16	6.454	17	7.091	4	9.414	24	36.953	6
Italy	6.471	28	4.155	44	5.184	27	2.745	26	9.479	22	28.035	28

(continued)

(continued)

2005–2010	Human capital		Market capital		Process capital		Renewal capital		Financial capital		NIC	
Mean	6.420		5.409		5.345		3.658		9.115		29.946	
SD	1.217		1.085		1.454		2.056		0.690		5.840	
Country	Score	Ranking	Score	Ranking	Score	Ranking	Score	Ranking	Score	Ranking	Score	Ranking
Japan	7.581	10	4.820	34	6.209	18	6.473	7	9.576	19	34.659	15
Jordan	5.345	37	5.341	26	4.411	32	2.212	30	7.865	45	25.174	33
Korea	6.964	19	5.123	29	5.282	26	4.595	19	9.383	25	31.348	22
Malaysia	6.538	26	6.410	9	5.567	23	2.186	31	8.740	35	29.442	24
Mexico	4.871	42	4.491	39	3.226	45	1.237	48	8.781	33	22.606	43
The Netherlands	7.312	12	6.761	4	6.879	10	5.163	13	9.739	7	35.855	10
New Zealand	7.123	18	5.999	15	6.460	16	3.701	22	9.380	26	32.662	21
Norway	7.936	5	6.055	14	7.008	7	4.961	15	9.987	1	35.947	9
The Philippines	4.772	43	4.464	40	3.317	43	1.268	47	7.481	47	21.302	46
Poland	6.393	29	4.246	41	3.895	38	1.819	35	8.945	30	25.299	32
Portugal	6.882	22	4.801	35	5.470	24	2.467	27	9.224	28	28.844	26
Romania	5.829	32	4.219	42	3.806	39	1.685	38	8.594	39	24.133	39
Russia	5.530	33	3.860	46	3.588	41	2.349	28	8.822	31	24.150	38
Singapore	7.144	17	8.306	1	7.506	2	5.416	11	9.961	2	38.334	5
South Africa	4.708	45	4.976	30	4.472	31	1.677	39	8.472	41	24.306	37
Spain	6.524	27	4.649	37	5.033	30	2.787	25	9.484	21	28.476	27
Sweden	8.385	2	6.563	7	7.174	6	7.780	2	9.673	12	39.575	1
Switzerland	7.575	11	6.481	8	7.374	4	7.988	1	9.753	6	39.172	2
Taiwan	7.244	13	5.823	17	6.026	20	5.425	10	9.526	20	34.044	18
Thailand	5.310	38	5.524	22	4.365	33	1.436	43	8.304	43	24.938	34
Turkey	4.703	46	5.227	27	4.167	34	1.666	40	8.690	36	24.453	36
United Kingdom	6.939	21	5.440	24	6.090	19	4.697	18	9.626	15	32.793	20
USA	7.695	7	5.348	25	6.558	13	6.715	5	9.886	3	36.202	7
Venezuela	4.884	41	2.761	48	2.545	48	1.277	46	8.625	38	20.092	48

Appendix 7
Country Profile: Additional Statistics

1. International Reserves in Millions of US$

Country	2005	2006	2007	2008	2009	2010
Indonesia	34,715	38,331	45,669	56,828	52,663	69,223
Malaysia	71,639	73,097	88,239	119,963	87,434	94,003
The Philippines	13,826	17,848	21,676	32,803	34,494	39,649
Thailand	47,535	53,709	69,100	107,469	113,743	141,084

Source: Global Finance http://www.gfmag.com/

2. GDP per capita–PPP Current international dollar

Country	2005	2006	2007	2008	2009	2010
Indonesia	3,207	3,449	3,727	3,987	4,155	4,394
Malaysia	11,380	12,274	13,278	14,024	13,733	14,670
The Philippines	2,935	3,130	3,383	3,515	3,516	3,737
Thailand	7,132	7,689	8,287	8,631	8,489	9,187

Source: World Economic Outlook Database http://www.imf.org/external/ns/cs.aspx?id=28

3. GDP (PPP)—share of world total_%

Country	2005	2006	2007	2008	2009	2010
Indonesia	1.24	1.25	1.26	1.30	1.37	1.39
Malaysia	0.53	0.54	0.54	0.55	0.55	0.56
The Philippines	0.46	0.46	0.47	0.47	0.48	0.50
Thailand	0.79	0.79	0.78	0.78	0.77	0.79

Source: World Economic Outlook Database http://www.imf.org/external/ns/cs.aspx?id=28

4. Gross domestic expenditure on R&D as a % of GDP

Country	2005	2006	2007	2008	2009	2010
Indonesia	0.04	0.05	–	–	0.05	0.05
Malaysia	0.63	0.63	0.64	0.57	0.72	0.84
The Philippines	0.14	0.11	0.12	0.1	0.1	0.1
Thailand	0.28	0.24	0.24	0.2	0.22	0.24

Source: IMD World Competitiveness Yearbook 2006–2011

C. Y.-Y. Lin et al., *National Intellectual Capital and the Financial Crisis in Indonesia, Malaysia, The Philippines, and Thailand*, SpringerBriefs in Economics, DOI: 10.1007/978-1-4614-7943-7, © The Author(s) 2014

Appendix 8
Fiscal Stimulus for Selected ASEAN Countries

Fiscal stimulus for selected ASEAN countries

Country	Amount (US$, billion)	Percentage of GDP
Vietnam	18.6	22
Malaysia	18.1	10.0
Singapore	13.8	10.7
Thailand	8.3	3.3
The Philippines	6.5	4.0
Indonesia	6.1	1.2

Source: Institute of Strategic and International Studies of Malaysia 2009 (Mei 2010)

C. Y.-Y. Lin et al., *National Intellectual Capital and the Financial Crisis in Indonesia, Malaysia, The Philippines, and Thailand*, SpringerBriefs in Economics, DOI: 10.1007/978-1-4614-7943-7, © The Author(s) 2014

Glossary

AIIF Asia Investment Infrastructure Fund

ASEAN Association of Southeast Asian countries (including *Brunei*, *Burma*, *Cambodia*, *Indonesia*, *Laos*, *Malaysia*, the *Philippines*, *Singapore*, *Thailand*, and *Vietnam*), China, and India

Basel II is the second of the *Basel Accords*, which are recommendations on *banking* laws and regulations issued by the *Basel Committee on Banking Supervision*. Basel II, initially published in June 2004, was intended to create an international standard for banking regulators to control how much capital banks need to put aside to guard against the types of financial and operational risks banks face

BBC British Broadcasting Corporation

Cap and trade Cap and trade is an environmental policy tool that delivers results with a mandatory cap on emissions while providing sources flexibility in how they comply

CIA The USA Central Intelligence Agency

CPI Consumer price inflation

ERP Economic resiliency plan in the Philippines

EU European Union

ETP Economic transformation program in Malaysia

ETS Emission trading system

FC Financial capital

FDI Foreign direct investment

GCI Global competitiveness index (published by World Economic Forum)

GDP Gross domestic product

C. Y.-Y. Lin et al., *National Intellectual Capital and the Financial Crisis in Indonesia, Malaysia, The Philippines, and Thailand*, SpringerBriefs in Economics, DOI: 10.1007/978-1-4614-7943-7, © The Author(s) 2014

GDP per capita (ppp) Gross domestic product per capita adjusted by purchasing power parity

HC Human capital

IMD International Institute for Management Development

IMF International Monetary Fund

IP Intellectual Property

Long-term NIC Long-term oriented national intellectual capital, represented by human capital and renewal capital

MC Market capital

MCC Millennium Challenge Corporation in the Philippines

MDGs Millennium development goals in Malaysia

NEDA National economic and development authority (the Philippines)

NIC National intellectual capital

OECD Organization for Economic Cooperation and Development

PBBC Philippine British Business Council

PC Process capital

Ppp Purchasing power parity

R&D Research and development

RC Renewal capital

Short-term NIC Short-term oriented national intellectual capital, represented by market capital and process capital

SMEs Small and Medium-Sized Enterprises

Term of trade Term of trade means what quantity of imports can be purchased through the sale of a fixed quantity of exports

TEVT Technical education and vocational training in the Philippines

Three time periods For the convenience of comparing ranking changes, the six years data were separated into three time periods, namely 2005–2006, 2007–2008, and 2009–2010. Two years each represents "before, during, and after" the 2008 global financial crisis. Even though Euro zone is still in sovereign debt trouble as of mid-2012, the time partition is based on the financial crisis progression in the epicenter. The signs of financial trouble appeared in 2007 and the crisis was declared over in the third quarter of 2009

UNCTAD United Nations Conference on Trade and Development

USPTO United States Patent and Trademark Office

VAT Value-added tax

WEF World Economic Forum that ranked Global Competitiveness Index (GCI)

WTO World Trade Organization

References

Abidin MZ, Rasiah R (2009a) The global financial crisis and the Malaysian economy: impact and responses, a joint report by the Institute of Strategic International Studies (ISIS) Malaysia and Faculty of Economics and Administration, Universiti Malaya commissioned by the United Nations Development Programme (UNDP). Retrieved from http://www.isis.org.my/attachments/456_The%20Global%20Financial%20Crisis%20and%20the%20Malaysian%20Economy.pdf

Abidin MZ, Rasiah R (2009b) The global financial crisis and the Malaysian economy: impact and responses. UNDP, Malaysia. Retrieved from http://www.undp.org.my/uploads/undp%20report%20-the%20global%20financial%20crisis%20and%20the%20malaysian%20economy.pdf

Adriyanto (2009) Coping with the global financial crisis: Indonesia's experience during 2008–2009, presented for Asian Parliamentary Assembly/session. Retrieved from http://www.fiskal.depkeu.go.id/2010/adoku/Adriyanto1.1.pdf

Balisacan AM, Piza SF, Mapa D, Santos CA, Odra DM (2010a) Social impact of the global financial crisis in the Philippines, Asian Development Bank. Retrieved from http://www.adb.org/documents/reports/social-impact-crisis-ph/social-impact-crisis-ph.pdf

Balisacan A, Piza S, Mapa D, Santos CA, Odra D (2010b) The Philippine economy and poverty during the global economic crisis. The Philippine Rev Econ (47.1):1–37. Retrieved from http://pre.econ.upd.edu.ph/index.php/pre/article/view/644/3

Bangko Sentral ng Philipinas (2009) 2008 annual report volume 1. Manila: Philippines ISSN 1655-5112. Retrieved from http://www.bsp.gov.ph/downloads/publications/2008/annrep2008.pdf

Bank Indonesia (2009) 2008 economic report on Indonesia, Bank Indonesia. Retrieved from http://www.bi.go.id/web/en/Publikasi/Laporan+Tahunan/Laporan+Perekonomian+Indonesia/lpi_08.htm

Bank Negara Malaysia (2009) Economic and financial developments in Malaysia in the fourth quarter of 2008, Ref. No.: 02/09/14. Retrieved from http://www.bnm.gov.my/view.php?dbIndex=0&website_id=1&id=690

Boediono (2009) 2008 economic report on Indonesia. Bank Indonesia. Jakarta: ISSN0522-2572

Bryant L (2011) Growth expected to slow in world's largest economies. Voice of America News. Retrieved from http://www.voanews.com/english/news/europe/OECD–Economic-Slowdown-Likely-to-Continue-129458543.html, 8 Sep 2011

Central Intelligence Agency (2012) CIA World factbook. Retrieved from https://www.cia.gov/library/publications/the-world-factbook/geos/id.html

Cheng W, Drilon C, Gagalac R (2010) Clinton, Aquino talk about anti-poverty programs, ABS-CBN News. Retrieved from http://www.abs-cbnnews.com/nation/11/10/10/clinton-aquino-talk-about-anti-poverty-programs

C. Y.-Y. Lin et al., *National Intellectual Capital and the Financial Crisis in Indonesia, Malaysia, The Philippines, and Thailand*, SpringerBriefs in Economics,
DOI: 10.1007/978-1-4614-7943-7,

Chirathivat S, Mallikamas S (2010a) Thailand's economic performance and responses to the global crisis. In: Proceedings of Asia after the crisis conference, March 5–6, Kyoto, Japan. Retrieved from http://ccas.doshisha.ac.jp/eng/Econference/econfpdf/26th%20Conference%20of%20the%20American%20Committee%20for%20Asian%20Economic%20Studies/Suthiphand.pdf

Congressional Research Service (1998) CRS report for congress: The 1997–1998 Asian financial crisis. Federation of American Scientists. Retrieved from http://www.fas.org/man/crs/crs-asia2.htm

Daly E, Singham S (2011) Jump-starting Malaysia's growth: An interview Idris Jala, Mckinsey Quarterly. Retrieved from https://www.mckinseyquarterly.com/Public_Sector/Economic_Policy/Jump-starting_Malaysias_growth_An_interview_with_Idris_Jala_2875

Edvinsson L, Malone MS (1997) Intellectual capital: realizing your company's true value by finding its hidden brainpower. Harper Business, New York

Exim Bank (2009) Research & planning. Brief Profile March 2009, Thailand. Retrieved from http://www.gnexid.org/country/Thailand.pdf

Global Finance (2012) Country Economic Reports & GDP Data: Thailand. Retrieved from http://www.gfmag.com/gdp-data-country-reports/163-thailand-gdp-country-report.html#axzz1lpkVjHiY

Guinigundo DC (n.d.) The impact of the global financial crisis on the Philippine financial system—an assessment in *BIS papers No. 54*. Monetary stability sector, Bangko Sentral ng Pillpinas. Retrieved from http://www.bis.org/publ/bppdf/bispap54s.pdf

Heritage Foundation (2012) Index of economic freedom. Retrieved from http://www.heritage.org/index/ranking

Hill H, Manning C (2009) Indonesia's new cabinet: boost for economic policy and reform. Aust Financia Rev. Retrieved from http://www.eastasiaforum.org/2009/11/02/indonesias-new-cabinet-a-boost-for-economic-policy-and-reform/

Ibrahim MB (2010) Impact of the global crisis on Malaysia's financial system in Bank of Malaysia. BIS papers No. 54. Retrieved from http://www.bis.org/publ/bppdf/bispap54p.pdf

IMF (April 2012) Regional economic outlook: Asia and Pacific, Managing spillovers and advancing economic rebalancing. Retrieved from http://www.imf.org/external/pubs/ft/reo/2012/APD/eng/areo0412.htm

ING Investor Dashboard Survey (2010) RP (Republic of the Philippines) Q3 investor confidence remains up—ING survey, GMA News. Retrieved from http://www.gmanetwork.com/news/story/203805/economy/rp-q3-investor-confidence-remains-up-ing-survey

Kehoe T (2010) The current financial crisis in Spain: What should we learn from the great depressions of the twentieth century? University of Minnesota and Federal Reserve Bank of Minneapolis, 18th Barcelona Lecture, Barcelona G.S.E. and Banc Sabadell, February 2010

Kritayanavaj B (2008) Global financial crisis 2008: A view from Thailand, World Urban Forum 4, 3–6 Nov 2008, Nanjing China

Kuroda H (2012) Asia to power world economy in 2012: ADB chief, The Economic Times. Retrieved from http://economictimes.indiatimes.com/news/economy/foreign-trade/articlelist/1200949414.cms, 26 Jan 2012

Lin CYY (2011) Leveraging intellectual capital for future competitiveness in Finland, Presentation at Tekes, Helsinki on 10 Nov 2011

Lin CYY, Edvinsson L (2011) National intellectual capital: a comparison of 40 countries. Springer Publishing Co., NY

Mah-Hui ML, Khoon GS (2010) The impact of the global financial crisis: the case of Malaysia. Third World Network Global Economy Series. Retrieved from http://www.twnside.org.sg/title2/ge/ge26.pdf

McCulloch N, Grover A (2010) Estimating the national impact of the financial crisis in Indonesia by combining a rapid qualitative study with nationally representative surveys. Institute of Development Studies. Retrieved from http://www.sed.manchester.ac.uk/research/events/conferences/developmenteconomics/papers/Mcculloch.pdf

Mei OS (2010) Global financial crisis: Implications on Malaysian economy. University Tunku Abdul Rahman. Retrieved from http://www.internationalconference.com.my/proceeding/icber2010_proceeding/PAPER_156_GlobalFinancial.pdf

Mendonça JR (2010) The impact of the international financial crisis on Brazil. Retrieved from http://www.realinstitutoelcano.org/wps/portal/rielcano_eng/Content?WCM_GLOBAL_CONTEXT=/elcano/elcano_in/zonas_in/international+economy/ari38-2010

Murniningtyas E (2009) Global financial crisis: Impact channels in Indonesia. In 3rd China-ASEAN Forum on social development and poverty reduction. Retrieved from http://www.adb.org/documents/events/2009/poverty-social-development/WG2A-impact-channels-Ino-Murniningtyas-paper.pdf

Nanto DK (2009) The global financial crisis: analysis and policy implications. CRS Report for Congress, Congressional Research Service 7-5700, RL34742, 2 Oct 2009

OECD (2010) Economic survey of Indonesia 2010, OECD. Retrieved from http://www.oecd.org/document/60/0,3746,en_2649_34571_46261052_1_1_1_1,00.html

OECD (2011) Southeast Asian Economic Outlook 2011/12. OECD Publishing. doi: 10.1787/9789264166882-en, Retrieved from http://www.oecd.org/dev/49427029.pdf

OECD (2012a) Philippines, in Southeast Asian Economic Outlook 2011/12, OECD. Retrieved from http://www.oecd.org/dev/49954093.pdf

OECD (2012b) Synopsis of structural policy challenges in Southeast Asia. In Southeast Asian Economic Outlook 2011/12, OECD. Retrieved from http://www.oecd.org/dev/49961978.pdf

Ortmans J (2011) Policy dialogue on entrepreneurship. Retrieved from http://www.entrepreneurship.org/en/Blogs/Policy-Forum-Blog/2011/October/Malaysias-Progress-with-Startups.aspx, 24 Oct 2011

Pak J (2011) Malaysia aims for hi-tech future, BBC News. Retrieved from http://www.bbc.co.uk/news/business-15475735, 27 Oct 2011

Philippine British Business Council–PBBC (2012) Philippine economy and 2012 outlook. Philippine British Business Council. Retrieved from http://philippinebritish.com/news/philippine-economy-and-2012-outlook

Reavis C (2009) The global financial crisis of 2008–2009: the role of greed, fear and oligarchs. MIT Sloan management case #09-093, published 22 Jul 2009

Reinhart CM, Rogoff KS (2009) This time is different: eight centuries of financial folly. Princeton University Press, Princeton. ISBN 9780691142166

Schwab K (ed) (2011) The global competitiveness report 2011–2012. World Economic Forum, Geneva

Singh A (2011) Asia–Pacific regional economic outlook: navigating an uncertain global environment, International Monetary Fund. Retrieved from http://www.imf.org/external/pubs/ft/reo/2011/apd/eng/asingh_manila.pdf, 17 Oct 2011

Tiongson ER (2010) The Philippines and the global financial crisis 2008–2009. Retrieved from https://docs.google.com/leaf?id=0B4yk7dFQf99vMTRmN2EwNTUtYWRlNi00ZDU4LTlm NmQtNmZmMzA1NWY5Zjg0&hl=en

Titiheruw IS, Soesastro H, Atie R (2009) Global financial crisis discussion series: Indonesia. Center for Strategic and International Studies, Overseas Development Institute. Retrieved from http://www.odi.org.uk/resources/docs/4327.pdf

Trairatvorakul P (2011) Thailand's economic outlook in 2011, Bank of Thailand, Opening remarks for the JSCCIB seminar. Retrieved from http://www.bot.or.th/Thai/PressAnd Speeches/Speeches/Gov/SpeechGov_21Jul2011.pdf, 21 Jul 2011

Verghis MA, Bhaopichitr K (2008a) Thailand economic monitor december 2008. World Bank Thailand Office. Retrieved from http://siteresources.worldbank.org/INTTHAILAND/Resources/Economic-Monitor/2008dec-tem.pdf

Verghis MA, Bhaopichitr K (2008b) Thailand economic monitor. World Bank Office, Bangkok. Retrieved from http://siteresources.worldbank.org/INTTHAILAND/Resources/Economic-Monitor/2008april_tem.pdf

World Bank (2012) Global economic prospects 2012a: uncertainties and vulnerabilities, World Bank Prospects. Retrieved from http://econ.worldbank.org/WBSITE/EXTERNAL/EXTDEC/EXTDECPROSPECTS/0,contentMDK:23064688~pagePK:64165401~piPK:64165026~theSitePK:476883,00.html, 18 Jan 2012

Yap JT, Reyes CM, Cuenca JS (2009a) Impact of the global financial and economic crisis on the Philippines. Philippine Institute for Development Studies, prepared for the United Nations Development Programme (UNDP). Retrieved from http://www.unicef.org/socialpolicy/files/Impact_of_the_Global_Finanical_and_Economic_Crisis_on_the_Philippines.pdf

Yap JT, Reyes CM, Cuenca JS (2009b) Impact of global financial and economic crisis on the Philippines. Philippine Institute for Development Studies, Discussion Paper Series No. 2009-30. Retrieved from http://www.unicef.org/socialpolicy/files/Impact_of_the_Global_Finanical_and_Economic_Crisis_on_the_Philippines.pdf

Yuvejwattana S, Heath M (2012) Thailand signals slower growth as export outlook wants: Economy, Bloomberg. Retrieved from http://www.bloomberg.com/news/2012-08-20/thai-growth-accelerates-as-domestic-demand-counters-global-woes.html, 20 Aug 2012

Zhuang J, Dowling JM (2002) Causes of the 1997 Asian financial crisis: What can an early warning system model tell us? In ERD working paper series No. 26, Asian Development Bank. Retrieved from http://www.adb.org/Documents/ERD/Working_Papers/wp026.pdf

Ziegenhain P (2010) Indonesia country report. In: Stiftung B (ed) Managing the crisis. A comparative assessment of economic Governance in 14 economies. Bertelsmann Stiftung, Gütersloh

Author Index

C. Y.-Y. Lin et al., *National Intellectual Capital and the Financial Crisis in Indonesia, Malaysia, The Philippines, and Thailand*, SpringerBriefs in Economics, DOI: 10.1007/978-1-4614-7943-7,

Subject Index

C. Y.-Y. Lin et al., *National Intellectual Capital and the Financial Crisis in Indonesia, Malaysia, The Philippines, and Thailand*, SpringerBriefs in Economics,
DOI: 10.1007/978-1-4614-7943-7,

MIX
Papier aus verantwortungsvollen Quellen
Paper from responsible sources
FSC® C105338

If you have any concerns about our products,
you can contact us on
ProductSafety@springernature.com

In case Publisher is established outside the EU,
the EU authorized representative is:
Springer Nature Customer Service Center GmbH
Europaplatz 3, 69115 Heidelberg, Germany

Printed by Libri Plureos GmbH
in Hamburg, Germany